We're (Nearly) All Victims Now!

We're (Nearly) All Victims Now!
How political correctness is undermining our liberal culture

David G. Green

Civitas: Institute for the Study of Civil Society
London
Registered Charity No. 1085494

First Published October 2006

© The Institute for the Study of Civil Society 2006
77 Great Peter Street
London SW1P 2EZ
Civitas is a registered charity (no. 1085494)
and a company limited by guarantee, registered in
England and Wales (no. 04023541)

email: books@civitas.org.uk

ISBN (10) 1-903386-53-5
ISBN (13) 978-1-903386-53-8

Independence: The Institute for the Study of Civil Society
(Civitas) is a registered educational charity (No. 1085494)
and a company limited by guarantee (No. 04023541). Civitas
is financed from a variety of private sources to avoid over-
reliance on any single or small group of donors.

All publications are independently refereed. All the
Institute's publications seek to further its objective of
promoting the advancement of learning. The views
expressed are those of the authors, not of the Institute.

Typeset by
Civitas

Printed in Great Britain by
The Cromwell Press
Trowbridge, Wiltshire

Contents

Author

David G. Green is the Director of Civitas. His books include *The New Right: The Counter Revolution in Political, Economic and Social Thought*, Wheatsheaf, 1987; *Reinventing Civil Society*, IEA, 1993; *Community Without Politics: A Market Approach to Welfare Reform*, IEA 1996; *Benefit Dependency: How Welfare Undermines Independence*, IEA, 1999; *Delay, Denial and Dilution*, IEA, 1999 (with Laura Casper); *Stakeholder Health Insurance*, Civitas, 2000; *Health Care in France and Germany: Lessons for the UK*, Civitas 2001 (with Ben Irvine); *Crime and Civil Society*, Civitas 2005 (with Emma Grove and Nadia Martin). He wrote the chapter on 'The Neo-Liberal Perspective' in Blackwell's *The Student's Companion to Social Policy*, (2nd edn) 2003.

He writes occasionally for newspapers, including in recent years pieces in the *Guardian* (on health reform), *The Times* (on race, NHS reform and crime), the *Sunday Telegraph* (on crime and victim culture) and the *Daily Telegraph* (on crime, immigration and welfare reform).

Preface

We have all noticed that terms such as racism, sexism, ageism, disablism, Islamophobia, and homophobia have become commonplace in public discussion. Like most people I have occasionally laughed at some of the more absurd uses of this language, but in recent years the politically-recognised victim status described by this list of 'isms' and phobias has begun to do lasting harm to our liberal culture. Moreover, the officially protected victim groups are no longer in the minority but add up to 73 per cent of the population.

Many were surprised to learn in June 2006 that the law now considers the murder of a gay man as a more serious crime than the murder of someone who is not gay. The murderers of Jody Dobrowski on Clapham Common were given 28 years when, according to the judge, if they had voiced no hostility towards the victim's sexuality, the sentence would have been halved. The case sparked some media comment. Was it really worse than the murder of medical student, Daniel Pollen, in Romford, Essex in July 2005—a killing that was captured on CCTV and appeared to be without obvious motive? The judge thought so in June 2006, and the 'starting point' for calculating the sentence of Daniel Pollen's killer will be only 15 years. Is animosity to gays a worse motive than, for example, a calculated killing to silence a witness—perhaps when a rapist murders his female victim to prevent her giving evidence? Or is it worse than a drive-by shooting that takes innocent life at random?

Singling out groups for special protection has had the inevitable consequence that others have begun to ask 'Why not us too?' Initially race was the only protected category when the 1998 Crime and Disorder Act created 'hate crime', but Muslim leaders complained and religion was soon added. Then pressure groups representing disabled people, as well as gays and lesbians, demanded to be included. The Government quickly agreed. Special legal status has now been given to four groups, and harsher penalties are available for crimes committed against individuals because of their sexual orientation, race, religion or a disability. But why stop at four? The Commission for Equality and Human Rights (CEHR), when it begins its work in 2007, will protect the same four groups plus two others, defined by gender and age. If the CEHR demands that crimes against women should also be officially classified as 'hate crimes', what intellectually coherent case could be made against it? And if members of Age Concern called for old people to be added to the list, what arguments could be used against them? Sooner or later, with only a minority of people outside the protected groups, we might ask ourselves what was wrong with the law before 1998? Is it not more consistent with our tradition of legal equality to believe that to murder or assault anyone, whoever they are, regardless of the group they identify with, is equally wrong?

We might go further and ask ourselves whether we have fallen into the trap that George Orwell warned about in *Animal Farm*—the corruption of the ideal of equality by power? Initially the 'seven commandments' on the farm wall included 'All animals are equal'. Later, the wall was repainted overnight leaving only one commandment: 'All animals are equal, but some animals are more equal than others'.

Some other episodes seem to fit the pattern. Groups who have been politically recognised as victims are starting to use their power to silence people who have had the cheek to criticise them. A phone call to the police by victim activists has led to people who have made perfectly reasonable contributions to public debate being warned off. Lynette Burrows, for example, argued that gay adoption was more risky for children than adoption by a married couple, and was questioned by the police. And so too was Sir Iqbal Sacranie who, while leader of the Muslim Council of Britain, voiced the disapproval of his religion for homosexuality. We may agree or disagree with these commentators, but if police power can be used to silence critics, have the victims becoming the aggressors, as Orwell warned? These are among the questions this short book tries to answer.

I am very grateful to Civitas researcher, Nick Seddon, for his assistance with chapter 3 and to Norman Dennis, Justin Shaw and Ken Minogue for their invaluable comments on all the chapters.

David G. Green

Introduction

To be a victim is to be harmed by an external event or oppressed by someone else, things that most people avoid wherever possible. Yet a striking feature of modern Britain is that many people want to be classified as victims. They do so because of the advantages it brings. Victimhood makes it possible to demand special protection in the workplace not available to other employees. It makes it possible to benefit from quotas, like the targets that require government departments to ensure that a defined percentage of public servants are from ethnic minorities. And it may be possible to demand that police powers are used against people who criticise you.

The word victim still retains its old meaning, and victims still inspire ordinary sympathy from kindly people. But today to be classified as a victim is to be given a special political status, which has no necessary connection with real hardship or actual oppression. Victimhood as a political status is best understood as the outcome of a political strategy by some groups aimed at gaining preferential treatment. In free societies groups often organise to gain advantages for themselves, but the increase in the number and power of groups seeking politically-mandated victimhood raises some deeper questions, as subsequent chapters will explain. Group victimhood is not compatible with our heritage of liberal democracy in three particular ways: it is inconsistent with the moral equality that underpins liberalism; it weakens our democratic culture; and it undermines legal equality.

First, the rise of victimhood as a strategy for gaining political power—that is, gaining control of the coercive apparatus of the state—is incompatible with Britain's heritage of liberalism. Why? Because it treats group identity based on birth, especially racial identity, as more important

1

than individual characteristics. This cuts into the foundations of liberalism, which seeks to release the best in individuals by freeing them from the constraints that might be imposed by their origins. Among the basic building blocks of liberalism is the idea that individuals should be judged by the personal qualities they can change and not by the characteristics ascribed to them by any accident of birth. To make assumptions about individuals based purely on ascribed characteristics such as parentage or race is to be prejudiced. Liberalism has insisted that individuals can rise above their circumstances. They can change, improve, or grow in skill and understanding. Consequently to attach paramount importance to ascribed characteristics today is to reverse hundreds of years of progress in triumphing over prejudice. The result has been to undermine a central component of liberalism: the sense of personal responsibility founded on moral equality, on which a free society relies. This concern is the subject of chapter 1.

Second, as chapter 2 discusses, the quest for preferential status has had a harmful effect on our democratic process and the political culture that nurtures it. In any democratic system there is a tension between two tendencies: majoritarian democracy and deliberative democracy. At its best our system is deliberative. Policies are made, not by gaining power and forcing decisions through, but by open debate that relies on modifying the opinions of others through the mutual learning that may emerge from listening and reflecting before deciding, a view classically expressed by Milton in *Areopagitica*: 'Let [Truth] and falsehood grapple; who ever knew Truth put to the worse, in a free and open encounter?'[1]

Victim groups encourage a majoritarian view, which emphasises gaining advantage at the expense of others through the use of the coercive powers of the state. We are used to interest groups pressing their case as part of a democratic process that allows opposing views to be accommodated through reasoned discussion and compromise. But modern victim groups create entrenched social divisions by defining opponents as oppressors who not only must be defeated by the state, but silenced by the state. It weakens the toleration and give-and-take that have been central to our political culture, and even encourages aggression. The underlying assumption of the growing culture of victimhood has been that one group is the victim and another is the oppressor: women are the victims of male discrimination; ethnic minorities of white discrimination; and disabled people of discrimination at the hands of the non-disabled. In each of these cases there is a commission with coercive powers to protect the victims: the Equal Opportunities Commission, the Commission for Racial Equality and the Disability Rights Commission. Moreover, victim status can insulate a group from criticism that would apply to anyone else. It does so by implying that all critics must be oppressors. The pseudo-psychiatric term 'Islamophobia', for example, suggests not simply that every criticism of Muslims is motivated by unreasonably exaggerated fear or hostility. It is a statement that any criticism of Muslims is evidence of clinical pathology. Yet, the label 'Islamophobic' is often attached to valid criticisms of particular Muslims whose behaviour has laid them open to legitimate censure.

Third, as chapter 3 considers, legal equality has also been undermined, in two senses. The creation of 'hate crimes' has weakened police and judicial impartiality. Some crimes are punished more severely when they are racially or religiously aggravated, thus treating the same crime as more serious when committed against a member of an ethnic minority than when it is committed against a white person. Second, anti-discrimination laws have been gradually transformed so that they are no longer confined to *prohibiting* discrimination against individuals because of their group membership; on the contrary, they facilitate and even call for, preferential treatment of people defined by their group identity.

The most troubling consequence of the emergence of rule by victim groups—'victimocracy'—is that we have become confused about the core elements of our own liberal-democratic culture. As a result, we have become weak defenders of our own precious heritage of freedom. Fundamental debates about moral equality, freedom and democracy have become confused in a fog of concern about avoiding offence even (perhaps most of all) to people who threaten us with violence. We are exhorted as individuals not only to show, but emotionally to feel, equal respect for both the core beliefs of liberalism and for rival ideas that are not compatible with a free society, even those that explicitly demand its destruction. These concerns are explained more fully in later chapters, but first let's look at the scale of the problem.

The scale

The number of protected groups is multiplying and the sheer scale has become a problem in itself. As time passes, there are fewer people left who are unable to claim victim status. From 2007, the government intends to establish a Commission for Equality and Human Rights (CEHR) that will protect six groups: the traditional three, plus those defined by sexual orientation, age, and religion or belief. In doing so, it continues a process begun in 1965, with the Race Relations Act, which led to the Race Relations Board in 1966, later transformed into the Commission for Racial Equality (CRE). The next landmark was the Equal Pay Act 1970, which came into force in 1975, when the Sex Discrimination Act also became law. The Equal Opportunities Commission (EOC) was established in 1975. Twenty years then elapsed before the Disability Discrimination Act of 1995, but it was not until 2000 that the Disability Rights Commission (DRC) was founded. The Equality Act 2006 established the CEHR, which starts work in October 2007 and includes the work of the DRC and EOC from that date. It will take over the work of the CRE by the end of March 2009.

How many victims?

Two calculations have been made: one based on the claim of some victim groups that they are subject to multiple discrimination (which has the paradoxical result that the total number of victims exceeds 100 per cent of the population) and one that avoids overlap.

Counting only the six official 'protected' groups we reach about 73 per cent per cent of the total population of the country, as Table 1 shows. The largest group is women, who make up 51 per cent of the population. The 2001 Census found that ethnic minorities make up about eight per cent of the population in total and that males comprise about half of all ethnic minority persons, or about four per cent of the total population. According to the Disability Rights Commission 48 per cent of disabled people of working age are female and 19 per cent of the population of working age are disabled.[2] Overall, the DRC claims that 22 per cent of the population are disabled and, assuming half are female, we need to add 11 per cent.

The other three categories are a little more difficult to calculate. Eighteen per cent of the population are pensioners, but the white paper on the CEHR also describes those aged 55-64 as subject to discrimination in the workplace. Moreover, it considers that people aged 16-24 can be disadvantaged in the labour market 'because of assumptions about their lack of ability and experience'.[3] However, I have only counted pensioners. In 2003 there were about 4.038 million males of pension age, some 6.8 per cent of the UK population. A further adjustment to avoid double counting ethnic minority males of pension age produces an estimate of 6.2 per cent of the total population, and a further adjustment to avoid double counting disabled people leaves 4.8 per cent.[4]

Table 1
Members of victimhood groups as a percentage of total population, adjusted for overlaps

	%
Female gender	51
Ethnic minority males	4
Disabled males (less ethnic minorities)	11
Male pensioners (less ethnic minorities and disabled)	5
Gay males (less ethnic minorities, disabled and pensioners)	2
Grand Total	**73**

Religion and belief are also not straightforward. Nearly 72 per cent of people said they were Christian at the time of the 2001 Census and 5.4 per cent belonged to non-Christian faiths. Strictly speaking, legal protection, applies to all faiths, and the term 'Christianophobia' recently put in an appearance, but it would be stretching credulity to declare that 72 per cent of the population were victims merely because they put 'CofE' on their census form. Assuming that half the non-Christians are males produces an estimate of 2.7 per cent, but most are from ethnic minorities and so I have made no addition for religion.

There are no official estimates of gays and lesbians and I have based the estimate of five per cent on the largest survey so far carried out in the UK, by the Wellcome Foundation, published in 1994 and based on a sample of 20,000 people.[5] To avoid double counting I have assumed that half are male (2.5 per cent) and made further reductions to avoid double counting ethnic minorities, disabled people and pensioners, leaving two per cent.

Allowing for multiple discrimination

If we take seriously the claim of some victim groups that they encounter 'multiple discrimination', the total number of victims adds up to 109 per cent of the total population of the country. This counter-intuitive result reflects the rise of 'identities' that allow many people to claim to be victims several times over. Stonewall, for example, claims on its website that 'a Black gay man might experience homophobia from parts of the Black community, racism from some parts of the gay community, and both racism and homophobia from everyone else!'[6]

Table 2
Members of victimhood groups as a percentage of total population, adjusted for multiple discrimination

	%
Female gender	51
Ethnic minority	8
Disabled	22
Non-Christian	5
Elderly	18
Gay or lesbian	5
Grand Total	**109**

How was the estimate of 109 per cent reached? 51 per cent of the population are women and ethnic minorities make up another eight per cent, according to the 2001 Census, and some 22 per cent of the population of Great

Britain are said to be disabled.[7] Eighteen per cent of the population are pensioners. And at the time of the 2001 Census about five per cent belonged to non-Christian faiths. A similar proportion were gays and lesbians.

1

Why modern victimhood is not compatible with liberalism

Our Tradition of Liberalism

Britain is a liberal democracy and, despite challenges, its guiding philosophy since the seventeenth century has been liberalism. Admittedly the term 'liberalism' is somewhat ambiguous, but there is no better alternative. John Locke encapsulated the essential ideas in 1689. His ideal might be called 'homeland liberty', because it is based on the assumption that a free people living in a particular land have come together to frame a system of government for themselves. Locke used the word 'commonwealth' to describe such an independent community of people: 'By *common-wealth*, I must be understood all along to mean, not a democracy, or any form of government, but *any independent community*'.[1]

Locke described the essence of the English heritage of law and how it differed from the more authoritarian Continental tradition. We should have a 'standing rule to live by, common to every one of that society' which meant, 'A liberty to follow my own will in all things, where the rule prescribes not; and not to be subject to the inconstant, uncertain, unknown, arbitrary will of another man'.[2] English law, in other words, was a method not only of exercising the power of the state, but also of excluding the state from various areas of social life—of protecting our right to use our energy, resources and time to improve our own lives and our shared institutions as we thought best. The law provided a clear warning when force could be used against us—and otherwise left us free. The tradition that has typically prevailed on the Continent is very different. Law is not a device for protecting the liberty of the individual, but rather a weapon in the hands of the authorities to enforce their will.[3]

Locke reminds us of the ultimate reason for valuing freedom. It is not so much that it has helped to make us prosperous but, above all, because it has institutionalised the moral equality of individuals. In our natural (by which he meant God-given, rather than pre-social) state, he said, there was equality, 'wherein all the power and jurisdiction is reciprocal, no one having more than another'.[4] All individuals were moral equals in the same sense that all are equal in the sight of God. If all were to come face to face with their Maker at the end of their lives, they must be allowed to take personal responsibility for choosing fact from error and right from wrong. Consequently, there must be freedom of study, thought, discussion, conscience and action. And government should, therefore, be based on consent.

At the beginning of the twenty-first century, hostility to homeland liberty comes from three types of collectivism: the first might be called 'patriotic' collectivism, the second 'cosmopolitan' and the third 'sectarian'.

Patriotic collectivism

The first variety of collectivism reflects the traditional animosity of authoritarians towards liberty. They want to put no serious limits on what the government can do, so that the hands of the authorities are not tied as they go about their purposes. Collectivism appeals to two main types of people: those who imagine they will be leaders, issuing instructions that are invariably said to be for the greater good; and those who are content to be led—sometimes only too glad to give their votes to leaders who promise to release them from all the main cares and responsibilities of modern life. Much welfare spending, for instance, is calculated to appeal to this group.

Collectivists make very different assumptions from liberals about what people are like and how a society is united. For collectivists, individual character and conduct are determined by social and economic conditions. Strictly speaking, deterministic theories imply that future events are inescapable, but in practice modern determinists believe that a few leaders can rise above economic and social forces. Societies are united, therefore, under the command of leaders who see things more clearly than the masses.

The liberal view is that people are moral agents, capable of exercising personal responsibility. They are united, not by leaders but by shared beliefs and commitments and their attachment to a political system based on equality under the law. Theirs is the social solidarity of people who expect a lot of one another and who demand much of themselves.

Collectivists usually put forward a well-established list of criticisms. The most common involve identifying themselves with the public good and liberals with its opposite. These claims boil down to three main assertions: liberals favour atomised individualism; liberals ignore the common good; and liberals favour unfettered selfishness or egoism. All can be rebutted.

Social atomisation was not defended by any mainstream liberal, such as Locke, Hume or Smith. How did the misunderstanding arise? Liberals were critics of the social order of their day, which was aristocratic and hierarchical. For them, in law and politics, people should be treated on their individual merits, not according to their birth. They especially objected to the idea of inherited social superiority. In that sense they were individualists, but their individualism took the form of belief in equality before the law, a social 'invention'. They knew only too well that shared beliefs and institutions were the bedrock of society. Justice, said Adam Smith was 'the main pillar that upholds the whole edifice',[5] but people should also seek to do right according to conscience: 'That the sense of duty should be the sole principle of our conduct, is nowhere the precept of Christianity; but that it should be the ruling and the governing one, as philosophy, and as, indeed, common sense, directs'.[6] These were not the words of someone who thought that we are all isolated individuals. On the contrary, the liberty of the individual guided by conscience was seen as a pre-condition for mutually beneficial social interaction. Liberal individualism was from the outset a theory of the individual in society: 'The liberty of man, in society', said Locke, was 'to be under no other legislative power, but that established, by consent'.[7]

Were liberals indifferent to the common good? Locke repeatedly uses the terms the common good and the public good throughout the *Second Treatise of Government*. It is true that he was suspicious of those who *pretended* to desire the common good, as was Adam Smith, but that was an objection to pretence, not the reality. The early liberals were suspicious of those who wanted to impose religious orthodoxy allegedly for the common good, but thought that justice and free enquiry were genuine public goods.[8]

Did liberals celebrate selfishness and look down on public altruism? Again, liberals were very far from celebrating untrammelled egoism. Blackstone, for example, writing about self-defence, said that the 'public peace' was a 'superior consideration to any one man's private property'. Moreover, if private force were permitted as a remedy for private injuries, 'all social justice must cease', because the strong would rule over the weak.[9] Locke's use of the term 'property' has given rise to the suspicion that he favoured 'property above people', but he uses the term to refer to the lives and liberties of individuals. In the language of the time, slaves were said to lack property in themselves. Far from celebrating egoism, Locke thought that 'Self-love will make men partial to themselves and their Friends'. Moreover, 'ill Nature, Passion and Revenge will carry them too far in punishing others'. Government was necessary 'to restrain the partiality and violence of men'.[10] Liberty was the right to do everything not prohibited by law, not the right to do anything whatsoever. As Locke famously insisted, liberty was not a 'state of licence'.[11] Adam Smith left no room for doubt about his own hopes:

> to feel much for others, and little for ourselves, that to restrain our selfish, and to indulge our benevolent, affections, constitutes the perfection of human nature; and can alone produce among mankind that harmony of sentiments and passions in which consists their whole grace and propriety.[12]

But why have I called the collectivists who advanced these criticisms of liberalism patriotic? Before answering that question, I need to explain what I mean by the two rival brands of collectivism, cosmopolitan and sectarian.[13]

Cosmopolitan collectivism

The main inspiration for cosmopolitan collectivism is disapproval of nationalism. For cosmopolitan collectivists, nationalism is synonymous with aggression towards foreigners. Such critics want nation-states to be replaced by supra-national institutions, which they contend will be more likely to encourage peace. Today, the utopian internationalism of the cosmopolitan collectivists attaches itself to the United Nations and the European Union.

But, as many writers have shown, there is no necessary connection between a legitimate love of the culture and beliefs of a particular country and aggression towards foreigners. George Orwell famously distinguished between love of country (patriotism) and hostility towards other nations (nationalism). More recently, philosophers such as David Miller of the University of Oxford have tried to restore the legitimacy of respect for 'nationality'—the beliefs and institutions that we hold in common and which work to the advantage of all.[14] In any event, there is no guarantee that a nation that surrenders some of its capacity for self-government to a supra-national agency will be less likely to engage in war than one that retains the ability to make its own laws.

Sectarian collectivism

The third fundamental critique of homeland liberty, sectarian collectivism—the topic of this book–is based on 'identity politics'. According to sectarian collectivists, all hitherto existing societies have been divided between victim and oppressor groups. Ideas such as impartial law or the common good are smokescreens created to conceal the power of oppressor groups. Some groups recognise themselves to be victims. Other groups suffer from a false consciousness of well-being and justice. In their case, better-informed sympathisers have to point out to them that they are oppressed and exploited.

Sectarian collectivism does not consist merely in forming groups to press for improvements or the redress of grievances; rather it demands political recognition for permanent victim status, entitling groups to special protection or preferential treatment by deploying the coercive means of the state.

Because their status is based on group membership, and because of the assumption that the politically salient characteristics of members are the same, absurdities and contradictions frequently arise for the reason that group members are not in reality all the same. For example, all members of ethnic minority groups that have successfully established their state-supported victimhood are taken to be victims and their oppressors are assumed to be whites. In reality, many successful and wealthy members of an ethnic minority can be much better off than many of the white people who are 'oppressing' them.

Multiculturalism is one of the variants of sectarian collectivism, or identity politics. The underlying idea is that all the cultural beliefs and practices associated with ethnic groups must be given equal standing with those of the host community, even if they are illiberal or incompatible with each other and with the culture of the host society. For example, demands are currently being made for political recognition of personal Sharia law, so that Muslim men with up to four wives can have their tax status recognised by Her Majesty's Revenue and Customs.

The underlying problem is treating group membership as the basis for political status. Historically, homeland liberty has been based on individuals. As we have seen, this does not mean 'isolated individuals', but it does mean that each person is in one sense alone as a moral equal. Originally this idea derived from the Christian view that all are the children of God and would one day be judged. Each person, whether rich or poor, therefore faced an obligation to lead a good life. This assumption of moral equality became a powerful argument against slavery, but also against theories attaching importance to fixed or ascribed social status. Liberalism from the time of Milton and Locke held that, regardless of the circumstances into which people are born, all must be free to lead their lives according to their conscience.

Modern identity politics, however, does not treat the individual guided by conscience as the main building block of society, freely entering into, or (more likely) resolving to uphold an already-existing liberal order for the public benefit. On the contrary, group membership is more important than individual characteristics. And the common good is not sought, but rather group advantage at the expense of others, who are defined as oppressors.

Multiculturalism can sound like a plea for pluralism. Words, of course, change their meanings. But 'multiculturalism' in its current sectarian-collectivist connotation of the equal status and worth of all cultures, and the desirability of a society being composed of many ethnic groups, is not at all the same as 'pluralism' in the sense established in sociology and politics during the twentieth century. Pluralism in the latter sense meant that, unlike the totalitarian societies of Nazism and Communism, society was not coincident with the state. In political theory, emphasis was placed upon a multi-party system as one of the hallmarks of a pluralistic society. People could move voluntarily from membership of a group when its codes and disciplines no longer corresponded with their own beliefs, preferences or needs. Pluralism meant that the law was silent about the practices of all groups that were acting within the confines of laws that allowed large scope for variety.

Once a measure of imperfect religious toleration was granted during the seventeenth century, for example, Catholics could take the view that the bread and wine were transubstantiated into the body and blood of Christ without fear of persecution and Protestants could treat them as mere symbols. The law neither approved nor disapproved of transubstantiation as a doctrine.[15] Before toleration, the law had required particular beliefs to be held, with killing the frequent result. During the sixteenth century the official requirements changed several times in quick succession as Henry VIII (who persecuted Catholics for heresy) was followed by Edward VI (who whitewashed churches and destroyed religious art to eliminate Catholic 'idolatry' as he saw it), then Mary Tudor (who persecuted Protestants) and then Elizabeth I (who fought against both Catholics and Protestant dissenters).[16]

Our laws have invariably tried to avoid giving a seal of approval to, much less coercive insistence on, particular lifestyles. Our laws largely prohibit harmful practices and otherwise leave us free. Thus, equal recognition until recently meant being left alone by the state—for the law to be silent on a wide range of beliefs and behaviours. Identity politics, by contrast, demands laws that bestow political recognition on certain beliefs and that authorise their state-enforced preferential treatment. Recent demands for schools to be legally obliged to allow Muslim girls to wear traditional Islamic costume, but all other pupils to wear school uniform, are but one example.

In the 1970s and 1980s, sectarian collectivism made significant inroads into the hitherto patriotic collectivist Labour party. Today, sectarian collectivism is associated with the left in politics. Sectarian collectivism—identity politics—had one idea in common with statists of the old Labour party who advocated nationalisation, extensive regulation and state welfare—namely antagonism to a liberal society. But until the 1970s mainstream Labour party members and leaders (as writers such as Norman Dennis have argued) were patriotic statists.[17] They thought the government should take the lead in bringing about reform and were inclined to glorify the state as embodying the best in people and to contrast the altruism of the public sector with the selfishness of the market. But, they wanted to change the country they loved—to build Jerusalem in England's green and pleasant land—not to destroy it.

By the 1970s the patriotic collectivists in the Labour party were losing out to elements that were antagonistic to the entire social order. The Trotskyites, an identifiable and familiar group wedded to the violent revolution of the international working class, achieved notoriety in the late 1960s and in the 1970s and 1980s. Their influence continued to grow in the Labour party until they were confronted by Labour leader Neil Kinnock from the mid-1980s onwards. Their strategy was essentially to inflame any dispute in order to expose what they saw as the hypocrisy of bourgeois society, or liberal-democracy as I have been calling it. Although much weakened by the 1990s, Trotskyites were still able to score occasional victories. Imran Khan, the solicitor representing the Lawrence family before and during the Macpherson inquiry, for example, stood as a candidate for Arthur Scargill's avowedly Trotskyite Socialist Labour Party at the 1997 General Election.[18]

Other beliefs, no-less hostile to the established liberal order, also took root in the 1970s and 1980s, especially identity politics that went wider than (and sometimes ignored altogether) the identity politics of working-class solidarity. Because the aim was to use political power to impose particular beliefs hostile to liberalism, it is properly understood as a variety of collectivism, but it was a divisive brand of statism, aiming to use government power to advantage one group over another. Like Marxists before them, these 'post-modernists' interpreted society as divided between oppressors and victims. But the victims and oppressors were no longer the non-affluent proletarian on the one hand and the capitalist, on the other: they were black versus white; woman versus man; disabled versus able-bodied; gay versus straight.

During the 1960s and 1970s Herbert Marcuse was the most influential voice, perhaps displaced now on the shelves of university libraries by Michel Foucault. Many of these pre-cursors of post-modernism were Marxists, from Gramsci onwards, who were trying to understand why the western white proletariat had failed to fulfil the revolutionary mission ordained to it by historical necessity. Their explanation was partly that the workers had been bought off by riches, but above all, that they had been deceived by the false consciousness their oppressors had succeeded in inculcating into them. Behind the façade of freedom and prosperity was the reality of a ruling elite who ran things to suit themselves. The task was to replace them by undermining the system through which they maintained control. The capitalist's control of the means of material production had not, as Marx had thought, been decisive. Rather the key to capitalist power was control over the means of 'mental production'—the education system, the mass media, and the socialisation of the child within the family of life-long matrimony. Revolutionaries should, therefore, take over the media, the entertainment industry, the arts and the education system. And the bourgeois family had to go. Most children acquired their subservience to the ruling elite from their parents, and so the loyalty of men and women to each other and their children through marriage must be weakened. What better weapon than the possibility of sex with many partners without the responsibility of children (made possible by contraception) or the risk of sexual disease (for a time naively assumed to be possible because of antibiotics)? The first steps of the long march through the institutions need not begin on the factory floor, but in the bedroom. Children brought up in fatherless families would be less sure of themselves, less attached to prevailing ideas, and consequently more vulnerable to the appeals of political activists. And if, in addition, their schools taught them that all ideas are of equal worth, because we have no way of judging the good from the bad, then young people would be far more easily manipulated by the new elitists who wanted to replace the old rulers. For a time these doctrines became the received wisdom of large sections of the intellectual left.

As part of a brilliant 'deconstruction' of the Macpherson report, Norman Dennis has succinctly explained some of the key post-modernist doctrines. According to Marcuse, revolutionaries should search for 'outcasts and outsiders' from 'the exploited and persecuted of other races and colours' as well as 'the victims of law and order' (that is, the criminals).[19] In the view of others, such as Adorno, they should try to free society from the domination of facts to reveal the truth as seen only by enlightened thinkers. They must fight 'the present triumph of the factual mentality'. For liberals, facts are great levellers that can be used by anyone, whether humble or mighty, to puncture the pretences of elites who think they know best. Yet, many intellectuals from the 1970s onwards were drawn towards the post-modernist critics of 'the factual mentality', who sought, by banishing statistics and other empirical findings from the argument, to make their own elitism impregnable to criticism. As such, their theories were no more than an excuse for their own brand of authoritarianism.[20]

This sectarian collectivism was sometimes closely allied with what I have called cosmopolitan collectivism, the doctrine of internationalists whose enthusiasm for international agencies over national democracies leaves no legitimate place for love of country. (Roger Scruton, turning the table on the 'phobia' phrasemongers, calls them oiks— people afflicted with the mental disease of oikophobia, the pathological fear or hatred of their own home.)[21] Though sectarian collectivism and cosmopolitan collectivism are otherwise distinctly different from one another, they are united in their hostility towards patriotism.

The Labour party is increasingly rediscovering the patriotic collectivism of the post-war Labour government.

This is the heritage with which Gordon Brown in particular seems to identify. Mr Blair's philosophy owes more to cosmopolitan collectivism, hence his support for the Human Rights Act, which treats national citizenship as of little relevance, and his passion for the European Union.

To sum up: the English heritage of liberty is based on the idea of an independent community of people understood as a kind of membership association that has founded a system of self-government to protect personal security, encourage open and representative government, and provide for individual liberty under the law. Personal security is provided by assigning the government a monopoly of force, which must be deployed according to law understood in a particular sense. There is to be a 'government of laws, not politicians' to prevent the arbitrary use of power; and the law must apply equally to all, to prevent favouritism. Open and democratic government is to be accomplished, not through majoritarian democracy, which implied enforcing fixed opinions, but by encouraging deliberative democracy—listening and reflecting before deciding. Individual liberty means being free to do anything not expressly prohibited by law, including the enjoyment of freedom of expression—and *a fortiori* the enjoyment of freedom of thought and attitude; the freedom to form, join and leave associations without the permission of state officials; and the right to leave the country and to move freely within it.

Sectarian collectivism puts no limits on potential uses of state power and is, therefore, incompatible with the rule of law. Moreover, it undermines equality before the law by supporting (as chapter 3 shows) legal reforms that have increased penalties for 'hate crime' and created ethnic quotas for public sector recruitment.

Victimhood is not compatible with moral equality

I have already argued that the core value of liberalism is the moral equality of individuals. It underpins the idea of equality before the law. It's easy enough to see why establishing a faction to gain advantage might lead to unfairness, but why claim that liberalism itself is threatened?

As some members of ethnic minorities have noted, seeking victim status can have a harmful effect on the victims themselves. Black American writers such as Shelby Steele have argued that it undermines self-respect.[22] But liberalism has always assumed a certain type of individual and a certain type of society. Individuals have been perceived as capable of bearing responsibility and of being inspired by the ideal of making a positive contribution to the advance of civilisation, perhaps modestly seen as 'doing your bit' or more grandly as aiming to emulate the greatest accomplishments of the human race so far. It was assumed that every facet of life could be improved and that all should play their part. Such individuals were not victims of circumstance, nor content to show obedience, let alone expected to show deference to superiors. They would make their way using their talents to the full, expecting hardships and pain and hoping they would have the strength of character to overcome them. *Pilgrim's Progress*, first published in 1678, and almost as widely read as the Bible until well into the twentieth century, summed up the ideal to aim for.

The tendency of modern victimhood to deny personal responsibility, however, is not the fatalism displayed by some religions. Victims are not said to be powerless in the face of God or nature. On the contrary, their oppressors are to blame for any unwelcome outcomes. Victims are never blamed—it's always someone else. As many writers have acknowledged, including Charles Murray in his impressive survey of *Human Accomplishment*, civilisation has advanced by individuals pushing themselves to the limit—pursuing 'transcendental' values: truth, goodness and beauty—not wallowing in self pity and delighting in blaming others.

The strong focus of liberal writers on the potential of individuals to change draws our eye to the most fundamental of all the building blocks of liberalism, the ideal of moral equality. It is the core value, the gut instinct, the visceral belief, so much so that we often get confused about how far to take it. Sometimes weight is attached to equal *outcomes* when to do so contradicts moral equality—the latter implies being able to make our own unique contribution and since we are all different it leads to different results. To suppress these outcomes is to suppress individuality.

A desire to sympathise with victims has also led us astray, particularly by encouraging a flight from personal responsibility. Victim status is closely allied with the medicalisation of life. Conditions like 'stress' have been re-interpreted as states of mind that can only be overcome with expert therapy or counselling. But they are further examples of the escape from personal responsibility. Another example is post-traumatic stress syndrome, previously understood as being upset after a serious incident like an accident. This condition too can only be resolved with help from highly trained counsellors, though financial compensation helps.

The result of this attitude is that genuine victims become less able to handle pain or loss. Instead of coping, they say to themselves, it should not have happened. And instead of digging deep within for strength, or sharing their problem with a friend or relative, the victim asks, 'Who is to blame and who should compensate me?' No one, it seems, should ever have to sacrifice anything, or struggle against adversity.

In America in the 1970s it became common to define black people as victims, and it was a white academic, William Ryan, whose book *Blaming the Victim*,[23] first published in 1971, supplied the catch-phrase still in common use. The new 'blame the victim' ideology, Ryan accepted, was very different from the old racism. Its adherents included sympathetic social scientists with a genuine commitment to reform, but they had been duped. Old racists believed that blacks were defective because they were 'born that way', but the emphasis on character and personal responsibility was not an improvement because it still located the explanation within the victim rather than in 'the system'.

For Ryan and similar academics, to assign any responsibility to a person was blaming the victim. All human conduct should be explained as the outcome of outside forces—the system. The public policy conclusion was that political power should be used to modify the 'outside forces'. He cites an activist friend of his who tried to do everything he could to generate citizen support for the welfare rights movement, including 'heartbreaking stories of life on welfare'. To Ryan's disgust, most of his listeners seemed 'unable to rid themselves of the ingrained belief that getting money without working for it—no matter how worthy and touching the recipient may be—is illicit, slothful and vaguely criminal'.[24] In Ryan's world-view, there was no place for such misguided qualms of conscience.

Ryan's argument appeals to our sympathy. Many American blacks were mistreated. No reasonable person could fail to condemn lynchings and the systematic denial of civil rights in the Deep South. But as inspirational leaders like Gandhi and Martin Luther King showed, it is how the victim reacts that matters most. They should not be quiescent; they should resist injustice, but in a manner compatible with a mutually respectful moral community. They should not replace the white man's hate with their own, but build a better world for all in order to maintain the values which allow diverse peoples to live together in peace. Martin Luther King's views were based on moral principles which could serve as a basis for freedom. He appealed to the best in people. Ryan appealed to the lower human instincts.

Moreover, in reality 'victims' may have contributed to their own predicament. If the remedy does, in practice, lie within the control of the victim then any observer should be free to say so. Traditionally many American blacks reacted to their situation by hard work, good character, thrift, self-sacrifice and family loyalty. As a strategy it worked, as the millions of American blacks who made it to the middle-class can testify, and as many black writers including Thomas Sowell and Walter Williams have convincingly argued. It also worked for Jews and many other ethnic groups in America.

We can gain greater insight into liberalism by comparing it with societies based on a combination of Islam and a tribal or clan social structure.[25] Liberalism implies a form of government based on the equal political status of citizens. Moreover, a liberal democracy is made up of individuals and voluntary associations, not clans or great families. It creates a sphere in which individuals govern their own actions. We each are assumed to have a political role in addition to a non-political, private or family life. Under liberalism, religion and the state are separate, with religion in the private sphere, whereas few Islamic societies separate the two.[26] Clan or tribal societies generally make no distinction at all between the political and private spheres. Equal status is also unheard of. The word of a woman, for example, counts for half that of a man in a typical Islamic court of law.

In a liberal society the law creates a private sphere where custom and moral pressure may hold sway but only in so far as they are the violence-free custom and moral pressure of a neighbourhood-community or voluntary association that individuals are free to leave for another community or association. In a clan or tribal society, however, there is only one sphere of control. Law must be obeyed under both liberal and non-liberal systems, but in a clan/tribal society customary social rules cannot be ignored either. In a liberal society a person may be born a farmer and become a scientist. There is the assumption, and to a large extent the reality, that individuals can change and improve. In the pure form of societies based on custom there is no such possibility. A daughter who flouts the will of parents may be killed, a practice mis-named 'honour killing' because it is said to uphold the 'honour' of the family. These ties have loosened in many contemporary societies, but they remain a force that cannot be ignored without risk.

As Larry Siedentop, in his neglected book *Democracy in Europe*, has argued, the main reason why Islam is so hostile to Western liberalism is that it senses the presence of Christianity behind it, a feeling that is entirely justified. Kant's universal guiding principle—'Act so that the rule of your conduct can be adopted by all rational agents'—was a secular version of the Christian injunction 'to love your neighbour as yourself'.[27] In Islamic societies non-believers are not equal under the law. And there is no question of loving neighbours who have left the faith. Moreover, Christianity emphasises conscience, whereas Islam typically demands submission or obedience.

The Christian claim is ontological—all are believed to be born to exercise judgement and to be guided by their conscience. Inequalities at birth are a fact, but no such status is permanent. No one is born to rule. And no one may be assumed to have superior knowledge without their claims being tested. Christianity has always emphasised conscience rather than mere obedience, a doctrine that ultimately led to governments based on liberal constitutionalism, which protected freedom of conscience for all. A government that protected all sects equally was preferable to the hope that your sect might gain control and impose its view by persecution. By the time of the Glorious Revolution in 1688, the lesson of the previous 150 years had been that the other sects were just as likely to take power. For everyone to abandon hope of being the persecutor was in the best interests of all. As Lord Acton claimed in his classic essay 'The History of Freedom in Christianity', the great achievement of the seventeenth century was for all sects to accept that toleration benefited everyone. The desire for freedom of worship was the 'strongest motive' in 1688, said Acton, and earlier struggles had taught that it was only by limiting the power of governments that the freedom of churches could be assured. That great idea, he wrote:

> teaching men to treasure the liberties of others as their own, and to defend them for love of justice and charity more than as a claim of right, has been the soul of what is great and good in the progress of the last two hundred years.[28]

The individual freedom offered by liberalism was, however, a demanding taskmaster. To do right an individual must sincerely choose the right course and not merely follow orders or comply out of fear. Slavish obedience without thought has generally been strongly frowned on by the Christian church. This is not to say that it is always unacceptable for an individual to follow the authority of church leaders and to hold beliefs as a matter of faith (that is without proof or the possibility of it), it is only to claim that an individual who is so inclined should accept the authority of a bishop or adhere to a faith as a conscious individual choice.

This claim, perhaps, requires, a little more defence. The Christian idea of conscience is not based on the idea of the completely autonomous individual, utterly separate from the wider society with its inherited customs and practices. It takes it for granted that there is a moral tradition contained in the Bible and the teachings of religious leaders, which should be taken into account by all believers. The idea of autonomy chiefly meant that unthinking obedience was not enough. Each was expected to conduct a moral struggle in the light of established authority, which was not fixed for all time, but open to interpretation. But just as scientists who hope to advance human knowledge must work with the methods for testing hypotheses recognised by their follow scientists, so religious believers are expected to accept public tests of 'truth for the time being'. In the Catholic church, for example, doctrine could change only by holding a council of bishops, but in more decentralised churches a simple meeting of the congregation might suffice. Moreover, the 'sacred text' also has a different status in Christianity compared with Islam. Under Islam, even modernist reformers regard the Koran as the verbatim word of God, whereas all but a handful of Christian sects regard the Bible as man's interpretation of the word of God, thus allowing for the possibility of earlier mistakes and leaving open the possibility of new interpretations in the light of changing events.

A liberal society permits groups to form for the pursuit of very different lives, including lifestyles based on obedience, but if membership of the group is not voluntary then its existence is not compatible with liberalism. A liberal constitution not only permits pluralism, it protects individuals who pursue a particular life, perhaps of self-transformation. It is taken for granted that no family or private group should be able to stop adults from following their own conscience. In clan societies, however, there is no private sphere in which individuals can go their own way. There is only time-hallowed custom to which obedience is due.

Thus, liberalism protects individuals from the state itself and from private wrongs and pressures, some of which may result from religious or ethnic solidarities. This means that there is a limit to what private groups can do to their members. Marriage, in particular, must be entered into freely. And each must be free to join or to leave their group. Muslims, however, are inclined to believe that people who abandon the faith of their birth are apostates who should be put to death.

Not all the protected identities threaten liberalism to the same extent. The variant usually called multiculturalism is the most dangerous. But by emphasising the group over the individual, all group identities weaken respect for moral equality and the sense of personal responsibility that goes with it.

To summarise: freedom for groups is not the same as freedom for individuals if the group does not respect freedom of conscience. Moral equality is the belief that every individual has the potential for rational autonomy and seeing right from wrong. From this view, it follows that people should not be treated differently solely because of inherited group characteristics—including race and gender, as well as the religion of parents and inherited status and wealth (or the lack of it).

2

Impact on democracy

The term democracy is often used as if it were unambiguous, but there is an important difference between 'majoritarian' and 'deliberative' democracy. In liberal countries constitutions have typically been enacted (or evolved in Britain's case) to both strengthen and limit public decision-making. We often speak of constitutional safeguards or limits as if the only aim were to curtail the power of government. Such limits have always been fundamental to avoidance of the abuse of power, but constitutions also seek to improve the quality of decision-making by requiring open discussion and building in delays to ensure that all points of view are heard and hasty decisions avoided. And as chapter 1 mentioned, some emotionally charged issues, especially concerning religious belief, have been kept outside the political domain to make it easier for debate to take place in an atmosphere of mutual learning through discussion and compromise.[1]

Behind the tradition of constitutional government are assumptions about the human condition, particularly the belief that all humans are fallible and that we need the help of others through open discussion to arrive at better judgements. In particular, liberals have mistrusted entrenched, hereditary power and wanted a constitution to create a sphere of personal security in which individual talent could thrive. Constitutions lock in safeguards against our worst selves to ensure deliberative democracy, that is learning through discussion, limits on power, and the exclusion of issues that can never be resolved by reasoned debate.

Earlier, I argued that modern victimhood is a political status that is sought after because of the advantages it brings. One consequence has been to weaken our democracy by encouraging a self-serving approach to the political process. Above all, seeking victim status encourages the invention and nursing of grievances. The underlying problem for victim groups is that once they have been given preferential treatment their power increases and, thereby, undermines the case for special treatment. As a result, some groups make strenuous efforts to maintain their victim status by exaggerating their sufferings. Four main strategies for gaining and maintaining victim status may be singled out: highlighting historic grievances; falsely claiming to have been 'insulted'; widening the definition of the group to increase political clout; and putting factual claims about their status beyond rational contradiction.

Highlighting historic grievances

The main criterion for victim status is that an oppressor imposes some kind of hardship. The most attractive hardships are those not experienced at all by the person laying claim to victim status or those suffered by someone else, which explains the appeal of historic grievances suffered by earlier generations. The wrong may have been real at the time, as it was with slavery, but ethnic minorities today may have suffered no direct ill effects from the eighteenth-century slave trade. Indeed, some will be descendants of the tribes who captured other Africans and sold them as slaves to European and Arab traders.

Increasing touchiness

Another opportunity is created by taking offence at innocent remarks or valid criticisms that are redefined as insults. This phenomenon explains the prevalence of speech codes. Feminists, for example, got away with claiming that words ending in 'man' excluded women. The term 'chairman' proved especially fruitful. It has been the custom for hundreds of years to address a male chairman as 'Mr Chairman' and a female as 'Madam Chairman'. The spelling never implied that only men could chair a meeting, but by claiming otherwise a grievance was invented and carefully nursed. The spelling of the word 'chairman' was proof of grievance in its own right and preferential treatment could be demanded without experiencing any real hardship or inconvenience.

One of the more perverse strategies has been to claim that living in a tolerant society is an insult. It takes the form of demanding not merely toleration for group habits, but equal respect. Thus activists among gay men say that they feel insulted if their behaviour in private is merely tolerated. Legal toleration is not enough and gay relationships must be put on an equal footing with heterosexual relations. In some ways the behaviour of such groups resembles that of adolescents in a bad mood. They are not going to be satisfied with anything less than total surrender to their will. An important part of the strategy is to establish that the victim is the sole judge of when language is offensive. To keep oppressors and sympathisers on the hop, every now and then they change the words that cause offence. Recently the use of the term 'mental handicap' has been redefined as insulting.

For many years a distinction was made between mental illness and mental handicap. The former was a condition that could be overcome through therapy and the latter one that could not. A person with a physically damaged brain, for example, will never fully recover. The pressure group the Royal Mencap Society however, prefers to use the term 'learning disability' and criticised the journalist Dominic Lawson for describing his own daughter, who has Down's Syndrome, as mentally handicapped. Mencap alleged that the term stigmatises people and Lord Rix, the president of the Royal Mencap Society, wrote to the *Independent* claiming that people with a learning disability regarded the term mental handicap with 'horror and disdain'.[2] The subject stimulated strong feelings and several 'letters to the editor' followed. One parent of a boy with a mental handicap argued that the term 'mental handicap' was 'an accurate and widely understood description'. We should, he said, 'use the correct term and dismiss the fabricated stigma'.[3]

Some gay activists have redefined the term 'homosexual' as an insult. Stonewall's web page on 'preferred terminology to use in media reporting' gives a list of approved words. The entry for 'homosexual' reads: 'Considered by some in the LGB community to be a derogatory and offensive term. It originates from a medical definition when same-sex attraction/relationships were construed as mental illness.' Instead, journalists are advised to use: 'gay, lesbian, gay man/woman, bisexual, bisexual man/woman or the acronym LGB (lesbian, gay and bisexual)'.[4] This criticism led the authors of a report for the Department of Constitutional Affairs to recommend that the term homosexual should be replaced in official documents.[5] Lord Falconer is reported to have accepted the recommendation.[6]

Stonewall in Wales has decided that the term 'openly gay' is unacceptable. In its web page on hate crime it warns journalists that 'Including phrases in reporting such as "the victim was openly gay" or somehow "flaunted her/his sexuality" suggests to readers that the victim is somehow responsible for the crime'. It suggests they 'brought it on themselves' and can serve to 'endorse some people's prejudices'.[7] However, the penchant of victim groups for changing at very short notice the words they find insulting not only traps oppressors, it can also catch out fellow victims. Word had obviously not got through to Stonewall in London, whose website displays the Stonewall manifesto for the 2005 general election. It regrets the fact that there are still only a 'tiny number of openly-gay MPs'. And the timeline of gay and lesbian history falls into the same trap when it says that 'Waheed Alli took his place in the House of Lords as the UK's first openly gay life peer'.[8] The Stonewall workplace equality index also uses the phrase and so does the equivalent web page of Stonewall in Wales, which endorses companies that have 'openly gay staff on their board of directors'.[9]

In some cases, the 'victims' themselves do not even ask for preferential treatment. Their champions have called upon local authorities, for example, to remove Christmas symbols to avoid insulting Muslims. However, spokesmen for Muslims had not requested any such sensitivity and expressed surprise that a local authority might think that way. In some cases it seems that secularist groups are seizing the opportunity to remove religious symbols from the public sphere, when the both Muslim and Christian leaders have an attitude of mutual tolerance.

Similarly, when a 10-year-old boy in Greater Manchester was taken to court by the police for racist abuse, the Muslim Council of Britain (MCB) said it thought it was unnecessary. Tahir Alam, chairman of the MCB education committee, was quoted in the *Daily Mail* as saying: 'With children as young as that we should work around these things so they develop respect for one another. The issue of racism is, of course, very serious but we should educate them, not take them to court.'[10] The action of the police appears to have been partly the result of a desire to improve the image of the police post-Macpherson.

Victim status can alter the balance of power in the work-place by making it more difficult for employers to object to conduct that is open to valid criticism. Ironically Sir Ian Blair, the Metropolitan Police Commissioner who has been one of the champions of political correctness, has found that his ability to manage gay or ethnic minority officers has been weakened. He recently moved Brian Paddick to another position and altered the management responsibilities of Tarique Ghaffur. The *Guardian* remarked that Paddick was the highest ranked openly gay officer and that Ghaffur was the Met's most senior ethnic-minority officer, and quoted George Rhodes, chairman of the Metropolitan Black Police Association, as saying, 'What message does this send about respect and reflecting diversity in the police service?'[11]

Category creep—getting in on the act

To gain political recognition it is necessary to build a coalition to put pressure on political parties. This need encourages groups to define themselves as widely as possible, to increase their voting impact. But it is not just that existing groups seek recruits, it is also that individuals who previously did not see themselves as victims change their attitude in order to profit. I recall a successful American business leader telling me about his mixed feelings about using his victim status. He was a Puerto Rican who had been very successful in America without playing the 'race card'. Yet, when his daughter was 18 he learned that he could get her into a better college if he highlighted her race. He believed in 'making it' on your own merits, but admitted that the temptation was too much and he seized the opportunity to benefit his daughter, despite his feelings that it was unjust.

Disability appears to have been most vulnerable to expansion. For many years disabled people, for example, had well-defined problems such as deafness, blindness or being confined to a wheelchair. In America, the process of 'category creep' has gone furthest, such that recovering alcoholics and obese people now claim to be covered by the

Americans With Disabilities Act. The British government was aware of the danger when the 1995 Disability Discrimination Act was passed and explicitly excluded by statutory instrument some potential disabilities, including 'a tendency to set fires', just in case arsonists tried to claim to be on a par with paraplegics. This expedient has not prevented recruitment reaching over one-fifth of the population.[12]

Putting factual claims beyond rational contradiction

When a group has a weak evidential case for its demands, it is common to try to downgrade the importance of evidence. One approach is to replace evidence with emotional appeals to distract attention from the lack of supporting facts. The claim that any criticism is 'blaming the victim', described in chapter 1, is one such ploy. In some cases the process resembles the invention of permanent victimhood, captured by words such as islamophobia, homophobia and disablism, which imply that the groups concerned are the constant victims of their oppressors. It takes for granted that someone is a victim when that is the factual claim to be established.

Another approach is to frame supporting arguments in terms that prevent factual contradiction, especially by asserting claims that cannot be tested. To assert the presence of prejudice or bias in human affairs as full proof of discrimination is one such device. But prejudice and bias are attitudes of mind. They are not actions and they may or may not lead to discriminatory actions. Whether or not there has been a discriminatory act in any particular case needs to be established. Unwitting attitudes of mind are even more useful. If the person with the attitude does not know he or she has it, how could anyone else know? And yet, the presence of such unwitting attitudes has been assumed to be a reality. Moreover, the possibility of 'positive' unwitting attitudes is neglected. For example, many people (unwittingly) are afraid of being accused of racism and bend over backwards to avoid giving offence. It is precisely this semi-conscious sense that is being exploited by protagonists for victim status. But, in any event, the law should always rest on demonstrated facts, not attitudes of mind—witting or unwitting.

The term 'institutional racism', as defined by the Macpherson Inquiry, provides one of the worst examples of putting issues beyond evidence. The Macpherson definition was this:

> The collective failure of an organisation to provide an appropriate and professional service to people because of their colour, culture, or ethnic origin. It can be seen or detected in processes, attitudes and behaviour which amount to discrimination through unwitting prejudice, ignorance, thoughtlessness, and racist stereotyping which disadvantage minority ethnic people. It persists because of the failure of the organisation openly and adequately to recognise and address its existence and causes by policy, example and leadership.[13]

The starting point for the Macpherson concept of 'institutional racism' is an outcome unfavourable to an ethnic minority. However, whether the outcome was *because* of their ethnic status is an empirical question that is assumed by this definition to be an established truth. This inadequacy is further compounded by talking of unwitting prejudice. But there may be prejudice without discrimination and it always remains to be established by investigation whether or not there has been either prejudice or actual discrimination.

It is worth unpacking some of this terminology a little more. The term 'prejudice' has two common meanings. One is to pre-judge without evidence or experience. The second is to form an adverse judgement about an individual or to treat an individual unjustly based on such pre-judgement. We inevitably make judgements about individuals based on their membership of a group, because some qualifications or types of behaviour are more common in such groups. It is a fact of human experience (and therefore not a pre-judgement) that group membership tells us something about individuals. Certain qualities are more common among the French than the British. People born to a certain culture are influenced by it. Someone raised as a Catholic in Italy, for example, is more likely to be against abortion than someone raised without religion in Soviet Russia.

As Norman Dennis has shown, such group general-isations, sometimes called stereotypes, are a useful and unavoidable part of the human condition. Prejudice, in its pejorative sense, is judging an individual in advance of experience or persisting with a judgement regardless of contrary evidence. For example, one group generalisation about the English might be that they are dry and unemotional. However, it would be an unjustified prejudice to insist that, because William Shakespeare was an Englishman, he must be dry and unemotional.

Stereotyping, says Dennis, is judgement based on 'experience of the *chance* that a person from this group or category is *more likely* to behave in one way than another'.[14] Such a view might also be called a bias, that is, an inclination towards a point of view or a preference for or against something. For example, we may be inclined to trust people who are well dressed rather than people who are scruffily attired. Our assumption could easily be mistaken but we have many momentary interactions with strangers when we have little option but to rely on such rules of thumb.

Our assumptions about group characteristics are general-isations that may or may not be true in particular cases. Moreover, as statistical generalisations they may be true of only a minority of group members. For example, a higher proportion of black Britons compared with white Britons have been to jail, but it's still only a minority of black men who have been imprisoned. The same would be true in America, but it did not stop black presidential candidate Jesse Jackson arguing that he had been reasonable when he was relieved to discover, on turning round in the street one dark night, that the footsteps he heard behind him were those of a white man. He had made an estimate of the risk of being attacked based on a group generalisation. He had not made a statement about all black Americans.

Stereotypes and prejudice are part of the human condition. A stereotype (based on a group generalisation) may be justified or not, and a prejudice (pre-judgement, whether adverse or not) may be unavoidable or not until direct experience can replace it. But both are attitudes of mind and, even when they exist, it still remains to be established whether or not discrimination occurred. Thomas Sowell gives an example from South Africa, where prejudice undoubtedly existed and laws explicitly prohibited the employment of blacks, but where the costs of *not* employing blacks were such that otherwise prejudiced employers hired them. The construction industry would have failed if building companies had not employed black workers. And in the Transvaal clothing industry all blacks were banned from working under apartheid laws, but in 1969 the majority of the workforce was black.[15] In these cases, then, there was prejudice and *legal* discrimination, but less *actual* discrimination than the law required.

Moreover, minorities may continue to flourish despite not only prejudice but also discrimination. Malaysia has restricted university access for the Chinese, but has been unable to impede their success. Throughout the 1960s, to give but one example, the Chinese minority were awarded over 400 degrees in engineering whereas the native Malays received only four.[16]

The important lesson is that we can avoid mistakes by basing our concern to avoid discrimination on evidence of actual behaviour and demonstrated outcomes. The mere presence of attitudes of mind is not proof of discrimination.

The consequences for democracy and constitutionalism

These stratagems for gaining and keeping victim status and the preferential treatment that goes with it have a harmful effect on our democratic system. Here are three such effects.

Weakening the ideal of limited government

Limited government is useful, not only because it defines the sphere in which the state can use legitimate force, thus leaving people free to improve their lives as they believe best in the remaining private domain, but also because it keeps heated issues, which are not easily resolved through the exchange of views or a spirit of compromise, outside politics. Victim politics tends to draw such contentious issues back into the political process with the result that it becomes more fraught and irrational.

Increasingly victim groups demand that hotly-disputed issues be made subject to police power. As described in chapter 3, differences of opinion about the best arrangements for adopting children have led to police action,[17] and so too have claims by Sir Iqbal Sacranie, then head of the Muslim Council of Britain, that homosexuality increases the risk of disease. In both cases, issues best resolved by the clash of opinion and the weight of evidence had been made a matter of force.

Many differences can only be handled, especially in a diverse society, by agreeing to disagree. Large realms of disagreement, especially in matters of faith, are not open to rational dispute, and are best kept outside politics. In the past, liberals argued that the best way to respect different points of view was for the law to be silent about them.

Undermines reason and mutual understanding

A further consequence of emphasising mutually exclusive group identities is that the potential to settle differences through reason itself is weakened. This problem is over and above the tendency to assert claims that cannot be tested, as touched upon earlier. I have in mind occasions when the non-victim is defined as incapable of understanding the plight of the victim: no white can understand the predicament of a black person; no man can comprehend the predicament of a woman. Any comment the outsider makes is unavoidably prejudiced and so the possibility of resolving conflicts by the exchange of views is ruled out.

The sensitivity that requires others to adjust to the self-defined sense of grievance of the victim is sharply in contrast with the morality of freedom Kant had in mind when he formulated the 'categorical imperative'. And it is not consistent with the 'golden rule' — do unto others as you would have them do unto you — which also enjoins us to take the feelings of others into account. For centuries, moral systems have urged us to try to see ourselves as others see us; to sympathise with the feelings of other people; and not to exempt ourselves from observing rules which apply to everyone else. But victim status justifies a quite different ethos. Only the victim can judge. This makes the sensitivity required very different from the ordinary civility expected in a typical daily exchange. Victim status is the perfect excuse for self-exemption from rules that rightly apply to others. It is not compatible with the mutual respect of free and responsible persons. The American lesbian feminist writer Tammy Bruce, who began to see some of the flaws in the intellectual positions she had earlier defended, has shown how many activists were motivated by what she calls 'malignant narcissism'.[18] That term may strike many as a little too severe, but she is right to emphasise that victimhood often focuses on the imperial self.

The wrong people benefit

A major side effect of victimism is that the wrong people benefit. Victim groups include a spread of different types of people. Some black Americans, for example, are rich and some poor. Because there is a higher concentration of poverty among black Americans compared with white Americans, privileges have been demanded for all blacks, including the rich. For example, quotas guaranteeing ethnic minorities access to universities have been enacted to compensate black Americans, but relatively few of those who have gained university places have come from poor backgrounds.[19]

Indeed, group privileges have often been harvested by the wrong people, that is the already-successful members of ethnic groups. For example, one of the mistakes made in America was to give preferential treatment to ethnically owned businesses as a strategy for alleviating poverty. Few consider it to have been a success. If anything, 'contract compliance' has benefited the already-successful members of minorities. Under the Small Business Act businesses owned by ethnic minorities were entitled to a proportion of government contracts. However, the American minority businessmen who were awarded these contracts were in no sense 'deprived'. They enjoyed a personal 'net worth' above that of all Americans.[20] Middle-class feminist women often make similar demands. They claim that women in the past have been discriminated against, and insist upon job promotions today, when they have personally suffered no loss and may not deserve on merit the job appointment they seek.

The assumption is made that the most important thing about a person is their group membership. Moreover, all group members are assumed to have had shared experiences, when they may not have done so. This assumption is significant because all group members can claim to have suffered hardships experienced by only a few members.

However, awareness that well-off people are using the political system to advantage themselves weakens confidence in democracy itself and encourages more people to take a cynical view of the public sphere. They may see it as less the domain for pursuing the common good and more the place to press your own interests—because if you don't others will.

Conclusions

I argued earlier that there is an authoritarian or anti-democratic dimension to the modern quest for victim status. Is this claim justified? Norman Dennis has succinctly described how doctrines that cannot be tested by any member of the public play into the hands of elitists who believe they have unique insights into social realities, sufficient to justify using political power to impose their view when they can. In the face of such claims, reliance on evidence is a great leveller; and the obligation to state factual claims in a way that anyone can test is a great equaliser.[21]

Liberalism emerged precisely as an antidote to groups who believed they had a special insight and a special right to control the 'ignorant' masses. Post-modernists who think they see social realities more clearly are, in this sense, no different from the champions of the divine right of kings, or aristocrats who thought they were born to rule. Authoritarians think that the arguments are already settled. The task is to act on the superior insight of the few, not to waste time questioning it. People must be moved to action, not given a licence to prevaricate. Liberalism's reply has always been: if you think you know something the rest of us don't, then submit it to the test of public criticism! Or in Popper's more exact vocabulary, state your theory in such a way that it can be refuted by evidence.

3

Victim status and legal equality

By requiring the consent of Parliament, following open discussion by all who might be subject to proposed laws, and by requiring that laws must apply equally to everyone, the intention of liberals was to reduce the risk that law would be abused to benefit particular groups at the expense of others. As Hume remarked in the eighteenth century, apart from purely personal loyalties three main types of political faction were found: based on affection (such as loyalty to a clan or noble family); principle (such as religious doctrine); or interest (such as a desire for monetary gain). Power had been constantly abused to benefit the favourites of the monarch, the religion favoured by the crown, and the landed or commercial interests with influence at court. The liberal alternative was for all members of society to seek only those laws that were for the good of all.

Historically, we have been accustomed to groups putting forward arguments for laws to be passed in order to give them an advantage. However, the expectation that law should serve the common good has generally made it necessary for anyone seeking private gain to claim that there is some public benefit involved. Manufacturers and traders, for instance, have not usually called for protection from competition so that they can make bigger profits, but to protect jobs and contribute to the prosperity of all. Even though some claims to act in the public interest have been false, nevertheless the idea that law ought to serve the common good has put limits on abuse.

In the modern era, laws privileging trade unions should have alerted us to the dangers of giving preferential treatment to organised groups. In 1901 the Taff Vale Railway

Company successfully sued the rail workers' union for losses suffered during a strike. As a result, the Liberal Government passed the Trade Disputes Act in 1906 removing trade union liability during strikes. Unlike everyone else, trade unions were henceforth able to break contracts without legal consequences. By the 1960s and 1970s trade union immunity was being frequently abused and by the late 1970s the legal protections given to trade unions in recognition of their weakness were widely seen as absurd. The victim had become the oppressor and, following a series of strikes in which union power was abused, the laws were repealed in the 1980s.

Despite this experience, preferential policies have been introduced in the UK, threatening the liberal ideal of equality under the law. But victim groups are not just political factions pressing for preferential treatment. They also undermine one of the fundamental building blocks of a free society, the equal legal status of its members. They do so in two main ways. First, laws have been enacted to award preferential treatment to some groups at the expense of others, not least laws setting targets for workplace recruitment. Second, the impartiality of the main criminal justice agencies, the courts and the police, has been weakened. For example, when ethnicity is involved, judges have been officially advised not to be impartial. And the creation of 'hate crimes' has led to the abandonment of the ideal of even-handedness in policing.

Weakening the impartiality of the police and judges

A booklet produced by the Equal Treatment Advisory Committee for the Judicial Studies Board, the official agency for advising judges, begins with the statement that: 'Justice in a modern and diverse society must be "colour conscious", not "colour-blind"'. And in order to emphasise the point, a list of nine 'do's and don'ts' includes: 'Be "colour conscious" not "colour blind"'.[1] But the police have gone the furthest. The laws against alleged 'hate crimes' have become a rationale for using police powers against innocent people who have had the temerity to venture an opinion disliked by a politically-defined victim.

Hate crime

The most pernicious developments have happened since 1998, when the law began to treat crimes against politically mandated victims as more serious than crimes against other individuals. Initially applied only to race, the number of victims claiming preferential treatment has grown rapidly.

In 1998 the Crime and Disorder Act[2] created the possibility that assault, harassment, criminal damage and public order offences could be racially aggravated. For example, the normal maximum sentence for common assault is six months. If racially aggravated, it is two years. Muslims objected that they were not specifically included (although, because most are Asians, they were covered as members of an ethnic minority) and so under the Anti-Terrorism, Crime and Security Act 2001, crimes could be 'religiously aggravated'. Moreover, the Powers of Criminal Courts (Sentencing) Act 2000, as amended, requires the courts to consider racial or religious hostility as an aggravating factor when deciding on the sentence for *any* offence that is not specifically racially or religiously aggravated under the 1998 Act. Soon the other organised victim groups were demanding preferential treatment and the Criminal Justice Act 2003 requires courts to consider disability or sexual orientation as aggravating factors when deciding a sentence for any offence.[3]

What have these legal changes meant in practice? There are two concerns. First, crimes against members of politically recognised victim groups are considered as more serious than those against other people. And second, police power has been used to suppress legitimate public discussion, under the guise of preventing 'hate crime'.

The Preface referred to the disparity in sentencing between a case in which the murder victim had been gay and another in which he had not. A similar disparity occurs when a murder victim has been killed on racial grounds. The 'starting point' for calculating the minimum sentence for a murder is 15 years, but it is 30 years when there is racial aggravation. The inequality was highlighted in summer 2005 when two terrible murders occurred on the same day in July 2005. Richard Whelan, a young white man, was murdered on a bus by a black youth who stabbed him several times because he asked him not to throw chips at other people on the bus. His murderer apparently carried a knife as a matter of course, but the murder was not considered 'racially aggravated'.

In the second case, Anthony Walker, a young black man of exemplary character from Liverpool, was stabbed with an ice-axe after he had been racially abused while waiting for a bus. The BBC was criticised for giving a great deal of air time to the murder of Anthony Walker and not mentioning the murder of Richard Whelan, so much so that it posted an explanation on its web site conceding that 'we should have mentioned the Whelan murder, however briefly'.[4] In November 2005 the murderer of Anthony Walker was given 23 years, after discounts.[5] At the time of writing the murderer of Richard Whelan has yet to be sentenced, but the 'starting point' will be 15 years, not 30. It is difficult to see why a murder on racial grounds should be considered worse than one motivated by sheer malice towards anyone who happened to irritate the perpetrator. As Detective Chief Inspector John MacDonald, who carried out the investigation into Richard Whelan's murder, said to the BBC: 'This was a totally unprovoked attack by someone who obviously carries a knife as a matter of course. Anybody could have been the victim of this crime.' The disparity is the result of the prevailing culture of victimhood and we urgently need to reinstate our long-standing commitment to equality under the law.

Of course, we have long recognised that all murders are not exactly the same. Killing in self-defence, for instance, has always been accepted. And the acceptability of some mitigating or aggravating factors is not in dispute. The problem is that we have weakened our commitment to equality under the law by relating aggravating factors to membership of victim groups, rather than to individual behaviour. We have fallen into the trap foreseen by George Orwell in *Animal Farm*: 'All animals are equal, but some animals are more equal than others'.

But sentencing is not the only problem, and the barrister Francis Bennion has described several cases in which the police have been used to intimidate people. The examples reveal the extent to which the leadership of the police has been captured by special interest groups who hope to use police power against their legitimate critics.[6] Some of the cases involving public figures have attracted press attention. Remarks about the Welsh by Tony Blair[7] and Christina Odone, for example, led to police investigations. When she was a panellist on BBC Question Time, journalist Christina Odone remarked during an exchange about Cardiff possibly hosting the 2012 Olympics instead of London that, from now on, the English 'are not going to be talking about the "leeks", and they are not going to be talking about the "little Welshies"'. A viewer complained about the latter phrase to the police who told Ms Odone during a telephone conversation that her comments constituted a 'race incident' but not a crime.[8] Although no punishment was meted out, the police had been used to intimidate her.

An even more blatant attempt to use the police to intimidate critics was made by Wyre Borough Council during 2005. Apparently in an effort to win the Navajo Charter Mark for Equality & Diversity, gay rights leaflets had been displayed on council premises. Mr Joe Roberts, aged 73, told the council that this offended his Christian beliefs, and he asked if he could display his Christian literature alongside the gay rights leaflets. The council reported Mr Roberts to the police, who came to his house. According to Mr Roberts:

> They warned me that being discriminatory and homophobic is in line with hate crime. The phrase they used was that we were 'walking on eggshells'. I asked the officer, if I phoned the police with a complaint that the council were discriminating against Christians would he go to interview them?[9]

A council spokesman said Mr Roberts and his wife Helen had 'displayed potentially homophobic attitudes' and admitted that the council had referred the matter to the police 'for further investigation with the intention of challenging attitudes and educating and raising awareness of the implications of homophobic behaviour'.[10] The police said they had given 'words of suitable advice' but, in truth, they had willingly been used to intimidate someone who was merely venturing a legitimate opinion in a free society.

How these events came about can better be understood by glancing at the guidance on hate crime produced by the Association of Chief Police Officers (ACPO). Its manipulative approach is revealed when the chapter on the legal framework says that it presents 'a number of legislative options to be used in combating hate crime'.[11] And later it gives links to 'legislative tools, which must be considered'.[12] A defender of liberty such as Locke (above) would never have called a law an 'option' or a 'tool'.

According to Peter Fahy, chairman of the ACPO Race and Diversity Working Group, writing in the foreword:

> Hate crime scars its victims beyond the legacy of any physical injury. If it is not professionally and successfully countered by the agencies of social control, its pervasive effect is to create alarm and fear as it chips away the mortar of social cohesion.

In a second foreword, Paul Evans of the Police Standards Unit, based in the Home Office, says:

> I would recommend Forces revisit their policies and tactical options particularly in relation to Repeat Victimisation with a clear emphasis on enforcement prevention and intervention at the earliest stages.

This plea for 'early intervention' seems to explain the police investigations that have increasingly hit the headlines. Among these, the 'gay horse' case is revealing.

Sam Brown was an Oxford undergraduate who went out in May 2005 to celebrate the end of exams. Emboldened by a drink or two he had said to a mounted police officer: 'Excuse me, do you realise your horse is gay'. Two squad cars were sent to arrest him. He was detained in a police cell overnight and given a fixed penalty notice for £80, which he refused to pay. The case came to court in January 2006 and the Crown Prosecution Service dropped the case at the last minute because there was not enough evidence to prove that his behaviour had been disorderly. The police disagreed and insisted that he had made 'homophobic comments that were deemed offensive to people passing by'.[13]

The police claim that the remarks were 'deemed' offensive had led them to charge him under section 5 of the Public Order Act with behaviour 'likely to cause harassment, alarm or distress'. The case reveals the major difficulty with hate crime, namely that facts do not matter. Ambiguity initially crept in when 'racist incidents' were said to be racist if somebody thought they were, whether their claim was true or not. The ACPO hate-crime document repeatedly states that the facts are immaterial. When speaking of secondary victimisation (when a person is dissatisfied with the police service) it says this:

> If, as victims of hate crimes or incidents, individuals experience indifference or rejection from the police this in effect victimises them a second time. Secondary victimisation takes place whether or not the police are indifferent or reject the victims if that is how the victim feels about the interaction. Whether or not it is reasonable for them to feel that way is immaterial. *The onus falls entirely on the police to manage the interaction to ensure that the victim has no residual feelings of secondary victimisation.*[14] (Emphasis in original.)

This mentality is not new and nor did it begin with the Macpherson report on the murder of Stephen Lawrence, as some have argued. Macpherson reported in February 1999 that the ACPO definition of a racist incident was as follows:

> A racial incident is any incident in which it appears to the reporting or investigating officer that the complaint involves an element of racial motivation, or any incident which includes an allegation of racial motivation made by any person.

Macpherson recommended replacement by a simpler form of words:

> A racist incident is any incident which is perceived to be racist by the victim or any other person.[15]

As Francis Bennion has shown, ACPO policy, reinforced by Macpherson, has removed the test that the law should expect conduct considered appropriate by a reasonable person. Bennion quotes the distinguished judge, Lord Macmillan:

> In the daily contacts of social and business life human beings are thrown into, or place themselves in, an infinite variety of relations

with their fellows; and the law can refer only to the standards of the reasonable man...[16]

Of course, these days a judge would refer to the reasonable 'person' not 'man', but the vital point is clear enough. By pandering to the desires of victim groups with an axe to grind, the police have stopped being the representatives of the 'reasonable person' and become the playthings of political activists or petty-minded members of the public.

There is now a considerable gulf between the rank and file of the police and their sociology-inspired senior ranks. Gradually, however, the recruitment strategy is replacing officers trained in the tradition of impartiality with those who have learnt how to demonstrate their gender or race awareness (or rather their 'diversity' awareness). In one recent case a 19-year-old female candidate for the police service had passed to the interview stage and was asked what she would do if she needed advice. She replied, 'I would go to my sergeant and ask him for help'. She failed the interview for saying 'him', thus revealing her lack of gender awareness.

Her treatment was the common experience of long-serving officers who began their careers in a service that upheld the view that the police should be even-handed — that justice was blind — but who now find they are treated like misfits in need of 'retraining' in diversity awareness. The new atmosphere was highlighted in 2002 at the annual conference of the Police Federation, when John Denham, the police minister, said that it was time to 'get down to the nitty gritty' on training of officers. His comment provoked a rebuke from PC Chris Jefford of the Met's training directorate. He told the minister that, if he used the term nitty gritty, he would face a discipline charge because the term was considered racist. PC Jefford said police had been told 'nitty gritty' was thought to have been a term used to describe slaves in the lowest reaches of slave ships.[17] The BBC subsequently included the term in its online e-cyclopedia, concluding that the origin of the term was obscure and citing experts who thought it had little, if any, connection with slavery.[18] But that had not prevented it from becoming a prohibited term in police circles.

The Racial and Religious Hatred Act 2006

The Racial and Religious Hatred Act was given royal assent in February 2006, but fortunately it was in a much weaker form than originally planned by the Government. Before its amendment in the House of Lords, the Government intended to enact a law that would have allowed the police to be sent in to silence individuals who criticised a religion, much as police power has been used to suppress critics of same-sex adoption or Islamic critics of homosexuality.

Our own history should have warned us of the dangers. The slaughter and disruption of Britain's own civil war, which ended with the execution of the King in 1649, turned the minds of many to the discovery of a political philosophy that would allow people who disagreed strongly nevertheless to live together in the same country. Among the main threats to this ideal of a free society were autocrats and theocrats. David Hume was among the most severe critics of religious leaders:

> We may observe, that, in all ages of the world, priests have been enemies to liberty; and it is certain, that this steady conduct of theirs must have been founded on fixed reasons of interest and ambition. Liberty of thinking, and of expressing our thoughts, is always fatal to priestly power, and to those pious frauds, on which it is commonly founded.[19]

Democracy has encouraged efforts to see the other person's point of view, to seek agreement rather than to quibble, and where possible, to compromise. For all groups to be subject to open criticism, including mockery and ridicule, has been a great leveller. In its original form the new law could have been used to persecute non-believers by dragging them through the courts, or to allow valid criticisms to be interpreted as incitement of hatred.

Due to the determined efforts of many members of the House of Lords, the Act was weakened, chiefly by requiring proof of intent to cause religious hatred and by inserting a clause protecting freedom of speech as follows:

> Nothing in this Part shall be read or given effect in a way which prohibits or restricts discussion, criticism or expressions of antipathy, dislike, ridicule, insult or abuse of particular religions or the beliefs or practices of their adherents, or of any other belief system or the beliefs or practices of its adherents, or proselytising or urging adherents of a different religion or belief system to cease practising their religion or belief system. (Clause 29J)

Given the willingness of the police leadership to allow politically-defined victim groups to deploy police power against their critics, clause 29J was a lucky escape.

Laws granting preferential status

The evolution of modern anti-discrimination laws

Modern anti-discrimination law began in the 1960s with America's policies to combat racial discrimination. The Civil Rights Act of 1964 was designed to prohibit preferential treatment of individuals according to race. It meant that individuals could not be advantaged or disadvantaged because of their group membership. Each must be treated as an individual, on his or her own merits.

However, the initial intention of preventing overt discrimination against blacks was soon being subverted. Like everyone else, black Americans experience some disadvantages not to their liking but wholly unconnected

55

with their ethnic status. The most damaging change occurred when public policies assumed *a priori* that every such disadvantage suffered by a black American was due to discrimination, regardless of other possible explanations. In particular, courts began to take it for granted that 'disparate impact' was evidence of discrimination. The underlying assumption was that if blacks were not represented, for example, in a workplace in the same proportion as in the locality in which the workforce lived, then it must be due to discrimination. The same reasoning was applied to other areas of life, such as university admissions and representation in senior management positions.

There are, however, many reasons why the representation of an ethnic group in a national or regional population would not be replicated in any given sub-division of society. From the beginning, fears were voiced that the law would be used to justify discrimination in *favour* of black Americans, rather than to prevent discrimination *against* them, but at the time of the Congressional debates about the 1964 Act such fears were dismissed. There had been an Executive Order passed by John F. Kennedy in 1961 using the term 'affirmative action' but it had been interpreted to mean that employers must be active rather than passive to ensure that job applicants and employees were treated in the same manner, that is 'without regard to their race, creed, color, or national origin'.[20] Alarm bells were sounded by a decision of the Fair Employment Practices Commission in Illinois early in 1964, which found that Motorola had discriminated against a black employee by requiring him to take the same test as other applicants for a job. When the case was raised during the debate about the Civil Rights Act, defenders denied that the new law would be interpreted to justify similar measures. Nevertheless, subsequent court decisions, including some by the Supreme

Court, did just that and accepted that discrimination had occurred if a measure, such as a test of ability to do a job, had a 'disparate impact' on minority groups. Similar developments have occurred in the UK, where the practice has been to describe 'disparate impact' as 'indirect discrimination'.

In one landmark American case in 1978, *Regents of the University of California v. Bakke*, Justice Harry Blackmun remarked: 'In order to get beyond racism, we must first take account of race,' and, he concluded that 'in order to treat some persons equally, we must treat them differently'.[21]

President Lyndon Johnson issued an executive order in 1965 that created the Office of Federal Contract Compliance. Nevertheless, it was not until 1971 that it issued guidelines laying down 'goals and timetables' to 'increase materially the utilization of minorities and women' with under-utilization defined as having fewer in a particular job type 'than would reasonably be expected by their availability'.[22] The idea has now been incorporated into British employment law. As well as prohibiting race discrimination in many public functions not covered by the original British 1976 Act, the Race Relations (Amendment) Act of 2000 placed public bodies under a duty to promote race equality. Listed bodies, in carrying out their functions, must have '*due regard to eliminate unlawful racial discrimination and to promote equality of opportunity and good relations between persons of different racial groups*'.[23] As the Office for National Statistics states:

> The duty means that, in everything they do, public authorities should aim to: eliminate unlawful racial discrimination; promote equality of opportunity; and promote good relations between people of different racial groups... The general duty does not say explicitly that you must monitor policy and service delivery. However, you will find it difficult to show that you have met your duty (to eliminate unlawful racial discrimination, and promote

equality of opportunity and good race relations) if you do not have any monitoring data... you should not assume that monitoring is something that you do not need to worry about.[24]

Much of the literature about public duties and targets is threatening in its tone but avoids watchwords like 'quota'. There are reasons for this linguistic ambiguity. Modood concedes that treating minority candidates 'differently from white candidates can be difficult to justify in any particular case, let alone to institutionalise through policies and procedures and to build the necessary consensus amongst managers, staff, etc.'. He is also aware that multiculturalism contradicts our basic 'intuition of fairness'. Both concerns mean that it will, therefore, be 'very difficult to get public support for differential policies that are not merely about tolerating difference but involve large-scale resource commitments'.[25]

In an effort to impose preferential policies while trying to make it look as if they are not doing so, the British Government has resorted to sheer doubletalk. Mike O'Brien, when he was Parliamentary Under Secretary of State at the Home Office, claimed that there was a substantive difference between 'targets' and 'quotas'. Following the findings of the Macpherson report, he wrote:

> ... these are targets rather than quotas. Quotas are illegal and are opposed by most of the minority ethnic communities. People are not looking for privileges or favouritism, merely an equal chance. Targets are about fairness, rewarding talent and putting an end to glass ceilings. Managers will have to deliver the targets or justify not hitting them in the same way as any other management target. They will be judged on their ability to deliver.[26]

But, if targets constrain the behaviour of managers, there is a clear departure from the ideal of recruitment solely according to ability to do the job.[27]

From 1999 the Government has set recruitment 'targets' for the Home Office to be achieved by 2009, with half-way targets by 2004. The Prison, Probation, UK Passport, and Immigration Services all exceeded their 2004 'milestones'. Office staff in London and Croydon were 38.3 per cent from ethnic minorities, well in excess of the 2009 target of 25 per cent. In 2005 the police achieved their 2004 milestone of 4.6 per cent and were progressing towards their 2009 target of seven per cent.[28]

Life chances, disaggregation and outcomes

Before focusing more fully on fallacious statistical reasoning, one further background assumption should be challenged: the idea that past outcomes for ethnic groups are reliable predictors of future prospects. We are used to the financial services industry warning us that past performance is no guarantee of future returns, but it is common to calculate the 'life chances' of individuals based on past experience. For example, what are the chances of someone from an ethnic minority working as a doctor in the NHS? A common approach would be to compare the number of ethnic minority doctors with the number of white doctors and to calculate the ratio. But this ratio is the result of past performance and may have no bearing on future opportunities. Nevertheless, it does not prevent commentators saying that if 33 per cent of NHS doctors were from an ethnic minority in a given year, the chances of future members joining the NHS are one in three. Such a statement disregards numerous factors that influence the outcome.

As shown below, there are many reasons for outcomes and we cannot assume that the causes of past occupational representation will remain the same. Whether or not there has been discrimination is an empirical question. Moreover, to speak of 'life chances' implies factors beyond the control of individuals, whereas some influences are under individual control and some are not. If the current pattern of representation were caused partly by factors under the control of individuals, then a change of attitude on their part —leading to greater imagination, energy, or determination— could make a difference to future outcomes. Their 'life chances', therefore, cannot be calculated by simply assuming them to be powerless.

Moreover, when comparing outcomes, it is important to compare like with like. Sowell shows that average black incomes in the US have been lower than for white Americans, but as far back as 1969, if blacks from homes with newspapers, magazines and library cards were compared, then they earned the same as whites from the same backgrounds and with the same educational attainments.[29] Similarly black professors earned more than whites in 1970 before affirmative action began, so long as variables such as published articles, ranking of the university that awarded their PhD and years of academic experience were held constant.[30]

These are examples of the importance of disaggregating groups so that the relevant causes of outcomes can be identified. The failures to disaggregate encourages sweeping generalisations about victim groups and makes testing factual claims difficult, if not impossible. But let's return to our main concern.

Statistical disparity is not proof of discrimination

Deliberate attempts to discriminate in favour of ethnic minorities are justified by pointing to the presence of disparities between the representation of ethnic groups in the total population and their representation in particular occupations. I argued earlier that such disparities are not proof of discrimination, but what are the reasons for doubting this common assumption?

The Prime Minister's Strategy Unit published a report in 2003 entitled *Ethnic Minorities in the Labour Market*, which looked at the role of 'human capital'—defined as the sum of skills, knowledge, experience and educational qualifications —in labour market outcomes.[31] The Strategy Unit found that some minority individuals possessed lower levels of human capital than their white counterparts, which harmed their employment opportunities. However, the Strategy Unit also discovered that, even when measurable factors such as levels of human capital and living in a deprived area were taken into account, people from minority ethnic groups continued to suffer an employment disadvantage:

> There are important and worrying disparities in the labour market performance ... that are not attributable to different levels of education and skills. The persistence of workplace discrimination is an important reason for this.[32]

In that last sentence the authors of *Ethnic Minorities in the Labour Market* fell into the trap of assuming that unexplained disparities must be the result of discrimination. No such conclusion is justified.

The underlying assumption is that the qualities and inclinations that make people suitable for an occupation are equally distributed between ethnic and cultural groups so that large statistical disparities would not arise without discrimination. Tarique Ghaffur, the assistant commissioner of the Metropolitan Police, for example, recently insisted that because there were 1.6 million Muslims in the country, 'there should be at least 20 Muslims in the House of Commons—not four'.[33] It is further assumed that statistical disparities are measures of such discrimination.[34]

Thomas Sowell has shown the weakness of this 'assumption about numbers'. 'Even in a random world of identical things,' he explains, 'to say that something happens a certain way *on the average* is not to say that it happens that way *every time*. But affirmative action deals with averages almost as if there were no variance.'[35] Moreover, the statistical methods unavoidably used to study ethnic representation leave much room for doubt. If the CRE, for example, were to survey 100 workplaces to test whether their workforce included eight per cent from ethnic minorities, it would have to ensure that its results were not purely random. Typically social scientists use significance testing to determine whether or not a result would have happened anyway, with or without discrimination. A common approach is to declare a 'confidence interval' such as 95 per cent. In such a case the result is assumed to be random in one in every 20 cases, so that if 100 workplaces were surveyed, there would be under-representation of ethnic minorities in five of them due to random chance, and quite apart from any other considerations. Sowell remarks ironically that you may be convicted of 'discrimination, even if you have only been guilty of statistical variance'.[36]

But in any event, it is not only that statistical methods are prone to error; when we consider the unequal distribution of personal characteristics within society as a whole, and within the ethnic groups that make it up, there are very good reasons to expect disparate outcomes. Dispro-portionate representation may be accounted for by many factors other than discrimination, including geographic distribution, personal choice, age, newcomer status, language, and cultural differences affecting the role of women and family structure.

Geographic distribution

Ethnic minorities now tend to live in Britain's major cities and conurbations. London is significant in that a tenth of all white people in the UK lived there in 2001 compared to almost half (45 per cent) of all ethnic minority people. A third of the population of inner London and a quarter of the population of outer London were from ethnic minority groups, after which the regions with the highest concentrations were the West Midlands at 11 per cent, followed by seven per cent each in Yorkshire and Humberside and the East Midlands.[37] Seventy per cent of black Africans and 61 per cent of black Caribbeans lived in London in 2001. More than half of the Bangladeshi group (54 per cent) also lived in London, while 21 per cent lived in the West Midlands, 20 per cent in Yorkshire and Humberside, and 16 per cent in the North West.[38] It is inevitable that the representation of minorities in particular workplaces (or leisure activities) will reflect this pattern. This reality, however, did not discourage claims in 2005 that under-representation of ethnic groups among visitors to the Lake District was evidence of discrimination.

Personal choice

There may be different attitudes in different ethnic groups towards what kind of employment is desirable. In 2002-03 some 16-18 per cent of Indian, Chinese, white Irish, and other non-British white groups were found in professional occupations. The proportion of Indian men working as doctors—a well-remunerated profession—is, at five per cent, almost ten times higher than the rate for all white British men. The groups with the lowest proportions of profess-ionals were the black groups, Bangladeshis, and Pakistanis, all with less than ten per cent. White British people also had relatively low rates of representation in professional occupations (11 per cent).

In 2002/03, 23 per cent of Pakistani and 18 per cent of Chinese people in employment in Great Britain were self-employed. This compares with around one in ten white British and fewer than one in ten black people.[39] Certain ethnic groups are concentrated in particular industries. In 2002/03, three fifths of Bangladeshi men and two fifths of Chinese men in employment worked in the distribution, hotel and restaurant industry, compared with one sixth of their white British counterparts. Pakistani men were the most likely to work in the transport and communication industry—25 per cent worked in this sector compared with ten per cent of employed men overall. Half of black Caribbean and black African women (52 per cent and 51 per cent respectively) worked in the public administration, education or health sectors.

These patterns have implications for career progression. It is often claimed that groups whose members on average occupy less favourable positions in the workplace have suffered discrimination. However, the Strategy Unit found that patterns of 'workplace progression reflect in part the nature of the industries in which certain ethnic minority groups are typically found'. [40] So the fact that 52 per cent of male Bangladeshi workers in Britain are in the restaurant industry, and a similarly high proportion of Pakistani workers are taxi drivers or chauffeurs, contrasts with the relatively high proportion of Indian medical practitioners. The first two occupations offer little or no opportunities for progression, whereas the reverse is true for the medical profession. This fact 'will influence, in very different ways, the career trajectories of Bangladeshi and Pakistani men on the one hand, and Indians on the other'.[41]

Age

One explanation for the low number of ethnic minorities in senior management is that people in such positions tend to be older. White groups have an older age structure than other ethnic groups, reflecting past immigration and fertility patterns. According to the 2001 Census, the UK has an ageing population. Taken as a whole, between 1971 and 2003 the number of people aged 65 or over rose by 28 per cent while the number of under-16s fell by 18 per cent.[42] The white Irish and white British groups had the oldest age structures of all in 2001, with almost one in four aged 65 or over.

As the Equal Opportunities Commission has observed, the relatively recent immigration patterns of some ethnic minorities mean that they are relatively young: for example, 38 per cent of the Bangladeshi population were under 16, double the figure for the white population.[43] As a function of natural growth rates, the Strategy Unit has projected that ethnic minorities will, between 1999 and 2009, account for half the growth in the working-age population.[44]

Newcomer status

Some ethnic groups include newcomers to Britain, who are likely to be at a disadvantage simply because the system is unfamiliar. Race may in this respect be irrelevant, since anyone arriving in a new country will find that many things—such as the customs, laws, or the endless form-filling—take some time to get used to. Among people living in the UK, the proportion born in the UK varied markedly by ethnic group. Other than the white British group, those most likely to be born in the UK were people from the mixed ethnic group and from the 'other black' group, 79 per cent in each. This reflects their younger age structure. A substantial proportion of the 'other black' group were young people who were born in Britain and who chose to describe their ethnicity as 'other black' and wrote in 'black British' as their Census answer. Black Caribbeans were the next most likely group to be born in the UK. Among the non-white ethnic groups, the older generations were less likely to have been born in the UK. For example, 83 per cent of black Caribbeans aged 25 to 34 were born in the UK, but only five per cent of those aged 45 to 64 were born in the UK.[45]

Language

The standard of a person's English is relevant to their success in jobs. It has an impact on the ability to fill out a job application form, and people without good spoken and/or written English are likely to find themselves at an initial disadvantage in interviews. The Policy Studies Institute (PSI) interviewed sample groups in the mid-1990s and found that 91 per cent of African Asians had a good command of English, compared with only 75 per cent of Bangladeshis and 76 per cent of Chinese. The fact is that while some ethnic minorities have higher qualifications than white people, 'some groups have significant groups who cannot speak English'. The PSI identified several factors, including sex, age on arrival, and the proportion of one's own ethnic group in one's neighbourhood, that 'have a bearing on fluency in English', and concluded, for example, 'that women of Pakistani and Bangladeshi origin, aged between 45 and 64, who have been resident in the UK less than 25 years and live in communities where more than ten per cent of residents are from a similar background, are the least likely of all ethnic minority groups to be fluent in English'.[46]

Perhaps a more definitive and up-to-date measure of linguistic aptitude is the one employed by the Home Office. It has found that 'in terms of educational attainment, irrespective of ethnicity, all pupils with EAL [English as an additional language] perform less well than those who have English as their first language'. There is a loose correlation between EAL children and those likely to come from low-income families, but for some minority ethnic groups the majority of pupils are registered EAL: over 90 per cent of Bangladeshi and Pakistani pupils, 82 per cent of Indians, 75 per cent of Chinese and 65 per cent of black Africans.[47] Many, however, do well in school despite this disadvantage.

Cultural differences

To what extent do cultural factors influence outcomes in schools and workplaces across the country? Tariq Modood, professor of sociology at the University of Bristol, blurs the boundaries between a fixed and unchanging ascribed status and a belief (chosen and open to challenge). He says that there are 'colour/phenotype racisms' and there are also 'cultural racisms' that 'build on "colour" a set of antagonistic or demeaning stereotypes based on alleged or real cultural traits'. The most important cultural racism today, he says, is Islamophobia.[48]

The American writer Orlando Patterson has exposed the inconsistency of writers who have tried to de-legitimise the importance of culture—but only when it suits their agenda:

> While Afro-American intellectual leaders, and all those who take a sympathetic interest in the plight of Afro-Americans, are quick to point to cultural factors in the defence of Afro-Americans against the onslaught of hereditarians, as well as nonracist conservatives, these very same leaders are equally quick to traduce, in other contexts, anyone who dares to point to the subcultural problems of the group in trying to explain their condition. It is now wholly incorrect politically even to utter the word *culture* as an explanation in any other context than counterattacks against hereditarians. Indeed, so far has this politically correct position gone that it is not uncommon for people who even tentatively point to social and cultural problems to be labelled and condemned as racists... We cannot have it both ways. If culture is a major intellectual weapon against the hereditarian racists, culture must contain the answers as we seek to explain the skill gap, the competence gap, and the wage gap, as well as the pathological social sink into which nearly a million Afro-Americans have fallen.[49]

Whenever we speak of race as a distinct characteristic of a person, it must involve some kind of genetic inheritance, whereas culture is the huge area of human activity—values, beliefs, customs, languages, habits, institutions—that is not genetically derived and has to be learnt. Anthropology has long accepted that a human baby taken from any community and placed in any other at an early age will learn the language, customs, and mores of the new family, regardless of racial characteristics. A liberal political culture is something that can be learnt by anyone, which implies that an individual can choose another culture. Those who blur the distinction between race and culture tend to assume that politics is or should be about promoting the interests of different racial groups, since there is no chance of different groups compromising by joining a common public culture. This is something that sectarian collectivists have in common with 'blood and soil' racists like the Nazis: they are hostile to a constitutional system based on a shared political culture, and want to replace it with a system based on loyalty to racial or sectarian identity. Modood falls into precisely this trap. He dismisses the argument of Trevor Phillips that we should nurture a British culture common to all races. Referring to the key elements of the common culture suggested by Phillips—the rule of law, democracy and fairness—he only says, 'yes, these things are great but we all know they can mean very different things. Democracy is a highly contested term.'[50]

Cultural differences between groups have an undoubted bearing on how likely the members of different groups are, on average, to succeed at school or in the workplace. As the Strategy Unit has acknowledged, 'the labour market successes of the Indians and Chinese show that the old picture of White success and ethnic minority under-performance is now out of date'.[51] For in reality, 'there are wide variations in the labour market achievements of different minority groups. Indians and Chinese are, on average, doing well and out-performing Whites in schools and in the labour market. Their success shows that there are no insuperable barriers to successful economic and social integration.'[52]

Gender roles and family structure are among the most important factors.

Gender roles: Gender differences reflect the culture of each group. For example, there is an enormous gap between the highest smoking group in society, Bangladeshi men (44 per cent), and the lowest, Bangladeshi women (one per cent), which is suggestive of the different roles played by men and women in that community.[53] Suicide rates are also revealing. Young South Asian women (the term is not differentiated enough, but is all we have), the Fawcett Society discovered, are particularly at risk of committing suicide, accounting for a proportion of suicides almost double their proportion in the population: 'It has been suggested that these women are likely to be experiencing problems which they do not feel able to discuss either within or outside the family'.[54]

By looking at the correlation between unemployment rates and economic inactivity (those not available for work and/or not actively seeking work), we see that Bangladeshi and Pakistani women had the highest unemployment rates; but Bangladeshi and Pakistani women also had the highest female economic inactivity rates at 77 per cent and 68 per cent respectively.[55] 'When asked the main reason for not being in the labour market', the Fawcett Society has found that the majority of Pakistani and Bangladeshi women replied 'looking after the family or home'.[56]

However, girls in every ethnic group, on average, perform better than boys at school. 'In each ethnic group, a higher percentage of 16-year-old girls than boys gained five or more A*-C passes at GCSE. Whilst 79 per cent of Chinese girls compared with 71 per cent of Chinese boys gained these qualifications, giving a difference of eight percentage points, for the lowest achieving group there was a larger gap of 15 percentage points between black Caribbean girls (40 per cent) and boys (25 per cent).'[57] While in the white population, the gender differences between men and women have been attenuated, it would be hard to argue the same for black Caribbean men and women—'the unemployment rate for men was high (15 per cent), the rate for women was much lower (eight per cent)'. The same can be said of Bangladeshi men and women—women's employment was very low at only 17 per cent, whilst nearly half of Bangladeshi men were in employment.[58] It must be possible that the relative status of the sexes within ethnic minorities may not have anything at all to do with discrimination by the majority white population.

Family structure: There are differences in the types of households different ethnic groups live in. Three quarters (74 per cent) of Bangladeshi households contained at least one dependent child in 2001. This was the highest proportion for any ethnic group and was nearly three times that of white British households (28 per cent). Households headed by a Pakistani or Indian person were also more likely than non-Asian households to contain at least one dependent child—66 per cent of Pakistani and 50 per cent of Indian households did so. White Irish households were least likely to contain dependent children.[59] Almost one fifth of Bangladeshi women in the UK have three or more children under 16, as do 16 per cent of Pakistani women, and nearly ten per cent of black African women. For all other women, including white women and black Caribbean women, the figure is 3-4 per cent.[60] Asians were more likely to have complex family structures, one measure of which is the number of households containing three or more adults with or without children. Such household structures make a large difference to the ability and willingness of members to work outside the family home. Some 17 per cent of white households were of this type compared with 49 per cent of those from Pakistan or Bangladesh.[61]

Family breakdown has an impact on the ability to get jobs. Not only is the ability of women to choose to combine employment and childrearing a significant issue,[62] it would not be easy for anyone, irrespective of background, to work, for example, as a full-time teacher or civil servant, while being a lone parent. At 45 per cent, the largest proportion of one-parent families is found among Caribbeans, compared with 21 per cent among whites and eight per cent among South Asians.[63]

Both Trevor Phillips and Tony Sewell of the Learning Trust, which runs the London borough of Hackney's education service, subscribe to a version of the 'cultural deficit theory', which says that African-Caribbean boys perform badly because of their domestic, social and cultural situation.[64] For Trevor Phillips, 'black children need role models and ideally parents, especially fathers, should play a more active role in their children's education'.[65] Dr Sewell has agreed with Mr Phillips that black men need to play an active role in the upbringing of their sons, since once boys hit puberty it is imperative that a father provides proper boundaries and guidance to counter under-achievement. As Dr Sewell has written, 'for too long in the fragmented family lives that prevail in black communities, a large number of black fathers have been allowed to evade this essential duty to their offspring. One central reason why Chinese and Indian children generally come top of school league tables is because they enjoy far more stable backgrounds than most white and African-Caribbean children.' It is, he goes on to say, substantially as a consequence of the absence of paternal role models that young black boys turn to gangland culture for a sense of male identity:

> Through its imagery and the lyrics of rap music, it has helped to create a nihilistic black youth culture that is anti-education and anti-achievement. There should be little surprise then that, in some classes, cleverness is not seen as cool. Successive ministers have failed to address these issues, preferring to hide behind the blanket pledge to tackle 'institutionalised racism'. This failure has been disastrous.[66]

To claim that the over- or under-representation of ethnic minorities must be caused by white discrimination is to ignore the impact of all these cultural factors.

4

Conclusions

So far I have argued that policies of preferential treatment for groups are incompatible with Britain's heritage of liberal democracy for three main reasons. First, because it undermines the bedrock principle of liberalism, personal responsibility grounded on the equal moral status of all. Second, because it encourages majoritarian rather than deliberative democracy. And third, because it infringes the ideal of equality before the law. But what are the underlying causes of politically mandated victimhood? Three can be discerned: group self-interest; misguided compassion; and political authoritarianism.

Is it right to think of victim groups as coalitions for the advancement of their own interests at the expense of other people? There have been, and are, real victims. American blacks, in particular, were badly treated historically. Has there been a multiplication of victims today because more people can genuinely claim to be oppressed? A diligent search produces little such evidence. And victim status undeniably brings sought-after advantages. Group self-interest includes not only material benefits but also emotional pleasures such as righteous indignation and exerting power over others. Demands to be able to subject opponents to police action are perhaps the strongest examples of the latter: 'I'll get the police onto you for saying that'. It may also be possible to demand compensation; it can justify preferential treatment in the jobs market; and it can put victims above criticism, a status especially useful to people who have laid themselves open to counter-argument. But there is a difference between victim groups and old-fashioned political coalitions for advancing private interests. Most such groups, including industry trade associations, seek protection or preferential treatment through lobbying and information campaigns, but they do not claim to be the victims of an oppressor. This linking of calls for preferential political action in favour of victims at the expense of their oppressors is a significant departure from normal interest-group lobbying because the sharp contrast between victim and oppressor deepens social divisions.

A second significant underlying cause of growing modern victimhood is misguided compassion—misguided because it neglects the harmful impact on the behaviour of victims and the wider consequences for society. Some people in society want to do good, partly reflecting their sheer good intentions, but also an element of self-interest. Public recognition of concern brings emotional rewards, which partly accounts for the prevalence of public displays of compassion, such as wearing ribbons in sympathy with this or that group. In some cases such displays can amount to a kind of personal therapy.

Nirpal Singh Dhaliwal has described the well-intentioned harm inflicted by teachers of black and Asian boys at an all-boys comprehensive in Ealing in the late 1980s. He was one of the boys:

> We'd often get a fresh-faced, idealistic teacher who had no doubt read Marx and Malcolm X and done an elective in post-colonial theory at polytechnic. We ate those suckers alive... Desperate to empathise with our persecution, they were knocked dead by our indifference and rampant misbehaviour. At the first sniff of guilt-ridden middle-class weakness, the feral instincts of teenage boys were unleashed and the class descended into anarchy. They thought we'd been crazed by oppression, so didn't want to come down too hard on us. They wanted to understand instead. When it did get too much for them and they threatened to march one of us to the headmaster's office, our immediate protest would be: 'You're a racist!'[1]

The boys despised the teachers who took the line that ethnic minorities had been oppressed and who concluded that wrongful behaviour in class should not, therefore, be challenged. Dhaliwal goes on to say that the teachers they respected most were strict, expected them to work hard, and ignored ethnic status. The author speculates that there are fewer such teachers today and that it is normal for teachers 'not to reprimand badly behaved black kids' because 'they suffer enough oppression as it is'.

The French writer de Tocqueville noticed the rise of misguided compassion as early as the 1830s. It happens when a kindly people become rich. Many people flourished under Britain's free constitution, but some did not, and the successful wanted to help the less fortunate. As a result, when Britain was the wealthiest country in Europe in the 1830s, it had the largest number of people on poor relief. In the end this misguided concern did more harm than good and reform of the poor laws followed, but the tendency continues to this day.

Not all rich countries have reacted with kindness towards disadvantaged members of their society. There is tremendous wealth in Saudi Arabia, but only a little reaches the poor, and so too in Russia, where wealthy oligarchs are more noted for prestigious spending on Western football clubs than for their philanthropy. But in Britain and other English-speaking countries, the supply of compassion has outstripped demand—we might say that there is a surplus of successful people looking for compassion outlets. It is a sign of the innate decency of the British people, but this social concern can be exploited. At the time de Tocqueville was writing about the poor law, and throughout the nineteenth century, there was a virtual industry of people who specialised in writing letters appealing for donations by inspiring pity. As a result, the term 'begging letter' took on the pejorative meaning that it retains today. In the nineteenth century kindness could be exploited because potential donors had little direct knowledge of the recipients of their charity. Modern efforts to seek victim status as a group appeal to the same cultural tradition, and rely on the same lack of direct knowledge and its replacement by 'sympathy', often at a safe distance and without thought for the real consequences.

Ironically, in their anxiety to prove their hostility to prejudice, especially racial prejudice, sympathisers end up by increasing its importance. In this country there has long been strong cultural disapproval of prejudice. We dislike being judged by our origins or other ascribed category. We like to be seen for what we really are, not judged according to some accident of birth. But paradoxically, despite the outward appearance of hostility to pre-judgement according to ascribed status, victimhood asserts that group membership is the primary identity of individuals. As Dhaliwal showed earlier, the 'racially sensitive' teachers of Ealing were more guilty of pre-judgement and stereotyping than the teachers who expected the whole class to work hard, regardless of race.

To suggest roles for self-interest and misguided compassion is probably less controversial than accusing some activists of authoritarianism, by which I mean hostility to liberal democracy. Is it not possible that they have failed to realise the consequences of their actions? Perhaps so, but if they persist in calling for the re-assertion of group identities and denying moral equality, and if they continue to undermine the legal equality of all, even after the consequences have been pointed out, we must credit them with knowing what they are doing. An earlier generation of socialists managed to combine a demand for equal outcomes with animosity to moral equality. Their calls for equalisation gave the impression of concern for the common person, but their real attitude was contempt. George Bernard Shaw, for example, said in *The Intelligent Woman's Guide to Socialism and Capitalism* that 'For my part I hate the poor and look forward eagerly to their extermination. I pity the rich a little, but I am equally bent on their extermination.' All classes including the working classes had 'no right to live: I should despair if I did not know that they will all die presently, and that there is no need on earth why they should be replaced by people like themselves'.[2] He was an unashamed elitist, and his attitudes did not die with him. No doubt there are many naïve champions of victim groups who think they are simply being 'nice', but it is no coincidence that many activists of the hard left who previously tried to inflame class divisions have switched their attention to victim groups as potentially more promising sources of hostility to liberalism. Their core belief is that they possess superior insights into the human condition and, consequently, are entitled to impose their will on others.

There is special danger in the variety of victimhood that demands equal respect for all group beliefs, as if none threaten the foundations of liberal democracy. But some beliefs, particularly Islamic precepts such as death for apostates or the inferior legal status of women, are not compatible with liberal democracy. If the core belief of liberalism is moral equality, then it assumes autonomous individuals guided by conscience and not merely obedient to authority. It contends that moral choice is only worthy of the name if it is a free choice, and that everyone, of any rank, must be considered capable of judging right from wrong. This is very different from the way that Islam is understood in many communities. According to a common inter-pretation of Islam, the first obligation is obedience. Many Muslims say that no interpretation of the sacred texts is permitted. Individuals can be punished for heretical opinions. Membership of the group is not voluntary and leavers may receive death threats. Individuals are not equal.

We urgently need to remind ourselves of the essential features of liberty so that we can defend it against subtle enemies. Liberty means living under equal laws intended to create the security to take personal responsibility for our own affairs. To be free is to be equal under law and to enjoy personal responsibility—the chance to follow your own plan of life. The founders of liberalism thought they were freeing every admirable human motivation. And they thought they were replacing the prejudice and bigotry that flourishes when knowledge is controlled from on high with open discussion to which anyone could contribute. They did not think all opinions were equally worth hearing, but that everyone should be heard so that the merits of their views could be judged impartially.

Victimocracy, as we see it emerging today, is not compatible with either liberty or democracy.

Notes

Introduction

1 Milton, J., *Areopagitica and Other Political Writings*, Indianapolis: Liberty Fund, 1999, p. 45.

2 DRC, *Disability Briefing*, June 2005.

3 DTI, *Fairness For All: A New Commission for Equality and Human Rights*, Cm 6185, May 2004, p. 14.

4 *Annual Abstract of Statistics* 2005, Table 5.3. About 22 per cent of people of pension age reported a long-term health condition or chronic illness. *Living in Britain 2000*, General Household Survey 2000, Table 7.13. London: TSO, 2001.

5 Wellings, K., *et al.*, *Sexual Behaviour in Britain*. London: Penguin, 1994.

6 www.stonewall.org.uk. Downloaded: 2 February 2006.

7 DTI, *Fairness For All: A New Commission for Equality and Human Rights*, Cm 6185, May 2004, p. 13.

1: Why modern victimhood is not compatible with liberalism

1 Locke, J., *Second Treatise of Government*, s. 133.

2 *Second Treatise*, s. 22.

3 For a discussion of our legal system see Scruton, R., *England: An Elegy*, London: Chatto & Windus, 2000, Chapter 6.

4 Locke, *Second Treatise*, s. 4.

5 Smith, A., *The Theory of Moral Sentiments*, Indianapolis: Liberty Fund, 1976, p. 167.

6 *Theory of Moral Sentiments*, p. 269.

7 Locke, *Second Treatise*, s. 22.

8 Milton, J., 'Second Defence of the People of England' (1652) in *Areopagitica and Other Political Writings*, Indianapolis: Liberty Fund, 1999

9 Blackstone, W., *Commentaries on the Laws of England*, vol. 3 , p. 4.

10 Locke, *Second Treatise,* s.13.

11 Locke, *Second Treatise,* s. 6.

12 Smith, *Theory of Moral Sentiments,* pp. 71-72.

13 For an excellent discussion see Conway, D., *In Defence of the Realm.* Aldershot: Ashgate, 2004.

14 Miller, D., *On Nationality,* Oxford: Clarendon Press, 1995.

15 Catholics remained under various legal disabilities until 1829, but did not need to fear for life and limb from the Glorious Revolution onwards.

16 During the seventeenth century before 1688, James I, Charles I and the Commonwealth struggled against Catholics and Protestant dissenters. During the Commonwealth Puritans destroyed religious art as Edward VI had done, to eliminate what they saw as physical distractions from purity of heart.

17 Dennis, N. and Halsey A., *English Ethical Socialism.* Oxford: Clarendon Press, 1988.

18 See below for discussion of the Macpherson report.

19 Marcuse, quoted in Dennis, N., *Racist Murder and Pressure Group Politics,* London: Civitas, 2000, p. 130.

20 Horkheimer and Adorno, quoted in Dennis, *Racist Murder,* p. 130.

21 Scruton, S., *England and the Need for Nations,* London: Civitas, 2006, Chapter 8.

22 Steele, S., *The Content of Our Character,* New York: St. Martin's Press, 1990.

23 Ryan, W., *Blaming the Victim,* 2nd Edn, New York: Vintage Books, 1976.

24 Ryan, pp. 284-85.

25 This is not intended to be a description of all Islamic societies. There is considerable variety, but it is a description of some such societies, for the sake of comparison.

26 England is bit of a misfit because the Church of England is the established church and, therefore belongs in the political domain.

However, being the established church has very little practical significance, and if the Church of England were disestablished tomorrow, few people would notice. Turkey, whose population is overwhelmingly Muslim, is also an exception because the state is secular. However, in practice the Turkish government exerts control over religious leaders when necessary.

27 Siedentop, *Democracy in Europe*. New York: Columbia Press, 2001, p. 191.

28 Acton, J., *The History of Freedom and Other Essays*, London: Macmillan, 1907, p. 52.

2: Impact on democracy

1 For an excellent discussion, see Holmes, S., *The Anatomy of Antiliberalism*. Cambridge, Mass: Harvard University Press, 1993.

2 *Independent*, 24 January 2006.

http://comment.independent.co.uk/letters/article340593.ece

3 *Independent*, 30 January 2006.

4 http://www.stonewall.org.uk/cymru/english/look_out/ resources_for_journalists/dictionary_of_equality_language/455.asp (Downloaded: 7 June 2006).

5 Healy, G. *et al.*, *Assessment Centres for Judicial Appointments and Diversity*, Report for the Department for Constitutional Affairs, March 2006, p. 54.

6 *Daily Mail*, 22 April 2006.

7 http://www.stonewall.org.uk/cymru/english/look_out/ resources_for_journalists/briefing_notes/471.asp (Downloaded: 7 June 2006).

8 http://www.stonewall.org.uk/information_bank/ history__lesbian__gay/89.asp (Downloaded: 7 June 2006).

9 http://www.stonewall.org.uk/cymru/english/workplace/ 642.asp (Downloaded: 7 June 2006).

10 *Daily Mail*, 8 April 2006.

11 *Guardian*, 2 June 2006.

12 DTI, *Fairness For All: A New Commission for Equality and Human Rights*, Cm 6185, May 2004.

13 Macpherson, W., *The Stephen Lawrence Inquiry*, Cm 4262-I, London: TSO, 1999, vol. 1, p. 28.

14 Dennis, *Racist Murder and Pressure Group Politics*, 2000, p. 140.

15 Sowell, *Applied Economics*, New York: Basic Books, 2004, pp. 175-76.

16 Sowell, *Applied Economics*, p. 185.

17 Bennion, F.A.R., 'New police law abolishes the reasonable man (and woman)', 170 JP (21 January 2006) 27.

18 Bruce, T., *The Death of Right and Wrong*, New York: Three Rivers Press, 2003.

19 See, for example, Sowell, T., *Civil Rights: Rhetoric or Reality?*, New York: Morrow, 1984, pp. 50-53.

20 Sowell, T., *Preferential Policies*, New York: Morrow, 1990, p. 158

21 Dennis, 2000, p. 131.

3: Victim status and legal equality

1 *Race and the Courts: A Short Practical Guide for Judges*, Judicial Studies Board, 1999. Cited in Green, D.G. (ed.), *Institutional Racism and the Police: Fact or Fiction?*, London: Civitas, 2000, p. 38.

2 Sections 29-32.

3 S. 146. Disability means any physical or mental impairment.

4 http://news.bbc.co.uk/newswatch/ukfs/hi/newsid_4730000/ newsid_4739300/4739389.stm

5 An accomplice received 17 years.

6 Bennion, F.A.R., 'New police law abolishes the reasonable man (and woman)', 170 JP (21 January 2006) 27.

7 His alleged insult of the Welsh was investigated by the police: http://news.bbc.co.uk/1/hi/wales/5167090.stm

8 *Sunday Times*, 9 April 2006.

9 Quoted in Bennion, 2006, p. 2.

10 Bennion, 2006, p. 2.

11 ACPO, *Hate Crime: Delivering a Quality Service*, March 2005, p. 12.

12 ACPO, 2005, p. 14.

13 *The Times*, 13 January 2006. Web:
http://www.timesonline.co.uk/article/0,,2-1982656,00.html

14 ACPO, 2005, p. 11.

15 Macpherson, 1999, vol. 1, pp. 313-14.

16 Donoghue v Stevenson [1932] AC 562 at 619; quoted in Bennion,
2006, p. 1.

17 *Daily Telegraph*, 15 May 2002.

18 http://news.bbc.co.uk/1/hi/uk/1988776.stm

19 Hume, D., *Essays, Moral, Political and Literary*, Indianapolis: Liberty
Fund, 1985, pp. 65-66.

20 Sowell, T., *Applied Economics*, New York: Basic Books, 2004, p. 187.

21 Cited in Bolick, C., *The Affirmative Action Fraud*, Washington: Cato
Institute, 1996, p. 46.

22 Sowell, T., *Civil Rights: Rhetoric or Reality?*, New York: William
Morrow, 1984, p. 41.

23 Race Equality Unit, *Race Equality in Public Services*, London: Home
Office, 2002, p. 6. Hereafter: '*Race Equality* (2002)'.

24 ONS, Ethnic Group Statistics, pp. 16-17.

25 Modood, T., *Racial Equality: Colour, Culture and Justice*, London:
IPPR, 1994, pp. 13-14.

26 O'Brien, M., 'The Macpherson Report and Institutional Racism,' in
Green (2000), pp. 33-34.

27 Green, D.G., 'Racial Preferences Are Not the Best Way to Create
Racial Harmony',
http://www.civitas.org.uk/pubs/racialPreference.php

28 Home Office, *Race Equality: the Home Secretary's Employment Targets*, sixth annual report, March 2006, p. 6; Race Equality Unit, *Race Equality: The Home Secretary's Employment Targets*, Milestone Report 2004, London: Home Office, 2005, p. iii.

29 Sowell, *Applied Economics*, p. 180.

30 Sowell, *Applied Economics*, p. 183.

31 Strategy Unit, *Ethnic Minorities and the Labour Market*, London: Cabinet Office, 2003, p. 27. Hereafter: '*Ethnic Minorities and the Labour Market*'.

32 *Ethnic Minorities and the Labour Market*, p. 4.

33 *Sunday Times*, 2 July 2006.

34 David G. Green, 'Liberal Anti-Racism', *Prospect Magazine*, October 2001. http://www.civitas.org.uk/pubs/prospectOct01.php

35 Sowell, T., *Civil Rights: Rhetoric or Reality?*, New York: William Morrow, 1984, pp. 53-54. Hereafter: 'Sowell (1984)'.

36 Sowell (1984), pp. 54-56.

37 Botcherby, S. and Hurrell, K., *Ethnic minority women and men*, London: Equal Opportunities Commission, 2004, p. 4. Hereafter: '*Ethnic minority women and men*'.

38 Summerfield, C. and Gill, B. (eds), *Social Trends*, No. 35, London: Palgrave Macmillan, 2005, p. 10. Hereafter: '*Social Trends* (2005)'.

39 Labour Force Survey, 2002/03. Hereafter: 'LFS (2002/03). http://www.statistics.gov.uk/cci/nugget.asp?id=463

40 *Ethnic Minorities and the Labour Market*, p. 24.

41 *Ethnic Minorities and the Labour Market*, p. 24.

42 *Social Trends* (2005), p. 7.

43 *Ethnic minority women and men*, p. 4. In fact, among ethnic minorities, the Mixed group had the youngest age structure, with 50 per cent under the age of 16.

44 *Ethnic Minorities and the Labour Market*, p. 4.

45 This is from the Office for National Statistics, *Focus on Ethnicity and Identity*.
http://www.statistics.gov.uk/cci/nugget.asp?id=459
The sources are the Annual Local Area Labour Force Survey 2002/03; Census, 2001, ONS; Census, 2001, General Register Office for Scotland.

46 Modood, T., Berthoud, R. *et al.* (eds), *Ethnic Minorities in Britain*, London: Policy Studies Institute, 1997. Hereafter: 'Modood (1997).' See also *Ethnic Minorities in Britain*, London: Commission for Racial Equality, 1999, p. 2.

47 *Race Equality* (2005), p. 28.

48 'Multiculturalism or Britishness: a false debate', *Connections*, Winter 2004/05, p. 9. *Connections* is the Quarterly Journal of the Commission for Racial Equality.

49 Patterson, O., *The Ordeal of Integration: Progress and Resentment in America's 'Racial' Crisis*, New York: Civitas, 1998, pp. 144-45.

50 Modood, *Connections* Winter 2004/05, p. 9.

51 *Ethnic Minorities and the Labour Market*, p. 13.

52 *Ethnic Minorities and the Labour Market*, p. 4.

53 *The Health Survey for England*, London: Department for Health, 1999.

54 Fawcett, p. 14.

55 LFS (2002/03). ONS:
http://www.statistics.gov.uk/cci/nugget.asp?id=462). See also Emily Brittain, *et al.*, *Black Minority and Ethnic Women in the UK*, London: The Fawcett Society, 2005, p. 18. Hereafter: 'Fawcett'.

56 Fawcett, pp. 19-20.

57 *Ethnic minority women and men*, p. 1.

58 *Ethnic minority women and men*, p. 14.

59 *Social Trends* (2005), pp. 21-22.

60 Fawcett, p. 4.

61 Modood (1997), p. 46.

62 Fawcett, p. 18.

63 Modood (1997), p. 41.

64 'Bad attitudes,' *The Economist*, 12 March 2005, 33.

65 CRE Spokesman on behalf of Trevor Phillips, 8 March 2005.
    http://www.blackbritain.co.uk/news/details.aspx?i=1274&c=uk&h=
    Black+boys+don%E2%80%99t+need+separate+classes

66 Tony Sewell, *Daily Mail*, 8 March 2005.

4: Conclusions

1 *Sunday Times*, 9 April 2006.
   http://www.timesonline.co.uk/newspaper/0,,176-2124987,00.html

2 Shaw, G.B., *The Intelligent Woman's Guide to Socialism and Capitalism*,
   London: Constable, 1928, p. 456.